Don Green

Rx: 521 PRESCRIPTIONS FOR LAUGHTER FROM A TO Z

Rib-tickling jokes, puns, stories and anecdotes are just the right medicine to enliven a talk or speech—or any conversation.

You'll find the right wholesome humor for any occasion in this complete sourcebook. It is thoroughly alphabetized and indexed to make it simple to find the perfect story to make a point in a good-humored way—or to create rousing laughter . . . just for the fun of it!

A TREASURY OF HUMOR

CLYDE MURDOCK

Zondervan Books • **Grand Rapids, Michigan**

A Treasury of Humor
Copyright © 1967 by Zondervan Publishing House

First printing January 1967
Second printing May 1967
Third printing April 1968
Fourth printing August 1968
Fifth printing September 1970
Sixth printing 1971
Seventh printing February 1972
Eighth printing June 1972
Ninth printing September 1972

Library of Congress Catalog Card Number 67-11611

Zondervan Books are published by Zondervan Publishing House, 1415 Lake Drive, S.E., Grand Rapids, Michigan 49506, U.S.A.

Printed in the United States of America

CONTENTS

(Numbers refer to stories)

We wish to acknowledge our appreciation to the following or permission to quote from their material:

McGraw-Hill Book Co., New York, New York, for the anecdote from *A Man Called Peter* (pages 164-165) by Catherine Marshall.

Abingdon Press, Nashville, for anecdotes from *400 More Snappy Stories That Preachers Tell,* by Paul E. Holdcraft, Parade Publications, Inc., New York, New York, for anecdotes from *Parade.*

The Rodeheaver, Hall-Mack Co., Winona Lake, Indiana, for anecdotes from *F'r Instance.*

Zondervan Publishing House, Grand Rapids, and Mr. W. E. Thorn for anecdotes from Mr. Thorn's book, *A Bit of Honey.*

ACCIDENTS—MISTAKES

1. *Experience*

A woman angrily jumped out of her car after a collision with another car.

"Why don't people ever watch where they're driving?" she shouted wildly. "You're the fourth car I've hit today!"

2. No *Confidence*

A cute young miss wanted her boy friend to be a hero. So after he was drafted he volunteered for the parachute outfit.

The instructor told him on the first jump to pull the cord with his left hand, after he jumped. But if it didn't open, then pull the other cord with his right hand.

"There will be a truck there to pick you up and bring you back," the instructor said.

The fellow jumped and pulled the cord with his left hand, but it didn't open. He pulled the other cord with his right hand, but it still didn't open.

He was heard to say, as he passed another parachutist on his way down, "Nothing works in this Army so far—and I'll bet the truck won't be there to pick me up either."

3. *Safety First*

The airlines company was disturbed over the high percentage of accidents, and decided to eliminate human errors by building a completely mechanical plane.

"Ladies and gentlemen," came a voice over a loudspeaker on the maiden voyage, "it may interest you to know that you are now traveling in the world's first completely automatic plane. Now just sit back and relax for nothing can go wrong ... go wrong ... go wrong!"

4. Not *Bragging*

The man was drowning. "Help, I can't swim. I can't swim!" he cried.

"I can't either," said the old man, sitting on the river bank chewing tobacco. "But I'm not hollerin' about it!"

5. Slow by *Comparison*

The young fellow was a chronic speed offender who

picked up two tickets a day from the motorcycle cop, one going to work and the other returning home.

Finally he bought a "souped up" foreign car, capable of traveling 150 miles per hour. Traveling home in it, at a speed of around 70 miles per hour, he was again accosted by the speed cop who pulled up along side of him to flag him down. Quickly stepping on the gas he pulled away from the motorcyclist and started traveling at 100 miles per hour. Eventually he slowed down, waiting for the motorcycle cop to catch up with him again. As the motorcycle pulled alongside, he pushed the pedal all the way down and took off at 140 miles per hour.

Becoming worried because he couldn't see the cop following him, he turned the car around and went back to look for him. To his surprise he found the cop crawling out from under his machine in the ditch.

"What happened to you, officer?" he asked the bruised and bleeding cop.

"Well," explained the police officer, "when you pulled away from me the last time, I thought my motorcycle had stopped, so I stepped off."

6. *Pessimism*

The driver of the automobile transport had his lights go out, so he turned on the lights of the top car on top of his truck, and kept on going. An approaching car veered sharply off the highway and landed in the ditch.

The transport driver ran to the driver of the wrecked car and said, "What made you go in the ditch?"

"Well," he said, "I thought if you was as wide as you was high, I would never get by."

7. All My *Fault*

Lady Motorist: "I'm afraid this accident was largely my fault."

Gentleman: "Nonsense! The blame rests entirely with me. I saw you at least three blocks away and had plenty of time to swerve down a side street."

8. Prediction *Predicament*

A local weather forecaster was so frequently wrong in his predictions that he became the laughing stock of the community. He, therefore, asked headquarters to transfer him to another station.

A brief correspondence followed.

"Why," asked headquarters, "do you wish to be transferred?"

"Because," the forecaster promptly replied, "the climate doesn't agree with me."

9. *Accidental*

A man decided to commit suicide. Saturating his body with gasoline, he put a rope around his neck, tied it to a tree limb, and put a pistol to his temple.

He then set a match to his body, jumped from the tree and pulled the trigger to the pistol.

Missing his temple, he hit the rope and fell in the water below. "If I hadn't been a good swimmer, I'd have drowned," he gasped, as he climbed back onto land.

10. *Precaution*

An old mountaineer was burying his wife, but on the way to the cemetery, as they passed a certain gate, she raised up from the casket, fully alive.

She lived several years and died again. On the way to the cemetery this time, as the family passed the gate, the husband said, "Now, boys, walk softly here. Remember, this is where she woke up before."

11. Abstain From *Appearances of Evil*

Mr. Jones picked the wrong umbrella in a hotel, and the owner called his attention to it. Embarrassed, he offered his apologies and went on his way.

The incident served to remind him that he had promised to buy both his wife and his daughter an umbrella, so he purchased them one each, along with one for himself.

Just as he was getting in the car with three umbrellas, he saw the man whose umbrella he had accidentally taken, eyeing him suspiciously.

The man said, "I see you had a good day after all."

12. Real *Appreciation*

A poor widow's son down in Texas, struck it rich with

oil, and as Mother's Day approached, made up his mind to show his appreciation by some unusual gift for all his mother had done for him. So he told the owner of a pet shop: "What is your most unusual and expensive pet?"

The merchant answered: "I have a Minah bird worth $27,000. It is the only one in the world that can recite the Lord's Prayer, the 23rd Psalm and the 13th chapter of First Corinthians."

"I'll take it," said the Texan. "I don't care how much it costs. Mom is worth it and she will get so much comfort hearing it recite Scripture."

So he bought it and shipped it off to his mother.

On Monday following Mother's Day, he called her long distance. "Did you get my bird?" he asked.

"Yes, son."

"How did you like it."

"It was delicious, son."

13. *Compromise*

A fellow was found with a rope around his wrist, strung from a light fixture.

His buddy cut him down and said, "What in the world are you doing?"

"Committing suicide!" he replied.

"Well, you should have put it around your neck if you really wanted to commit suicide."

The fellow answered, "I tried it around my neck but it was choking me."

14. *Glad* You're Here

Governor Al Smith, soon after he had been elected governor of New York State, visited Sing Sing Prison. He was asked to have lunch and after lunch to say a few words to the prisoners.

He cleared his throat and said, "Fellow Democrats" ... but he quickly caught himself, knowing no good Democrat should be in prison.

He started again: "Fellow citizens," but caught himself again suddenly, knowing that criminals often lost their citizenship.

He backed up and said, *"My friends*, I'm glad to see you all here."

15. *Goofed*

It was the first part in five years that he had managed to get in any play. True, it was only a small speaking part, but it was a start. The hero was to come on the scene and say: "Did you see this man get killed?" His part was simply to look the hero straight in the eyes and answer, "I did."

For weeks he practiced with those two words, studying elocution, practicing facial expressions and intonations. Then came the big day. The hero walked in, glanced at the body on the floor, looked at the actor and asked: "Did you see this man get killed?"

Looking full into the eyes of the hero, he answered clearly, "Did I?"

16. Get What You *Pay* For

A young man brought a cheap watch to the jewelry store to be repaired.

"I sure made a mistake in dropping my watch," he said.

The jeweler looked at it and said, "No, you couldn't help dropping it, but you sure made a mistake in picking it up."

17. Over *Introduced*

The sweet young miss came to the judge's office, tearfully pleading to be released from the three-day waiting period required by the state before marriage.

When asked the reason, she replied, "I've just been introduced to him and they tell me he's just the greatest guy."

Permission was granted.

Next week she returned to the judge's office, seeking a divorce.

"But you only got married last week," said the judge.

"I know," she said sorrowfully, "he is the most *over introduced* man I ever met."

18. Good *Behavior*

Mrs. Jones' son was coming home from prison, after serving a long sentence. Her neighbor, Mrs. Brown, said, "I thought he had another year to serve."

"Oh, no. He got off for good behavior."

Mrs. Brown, enthusiastically, "Oh, it must be a consolation to know you have such *a good son.*"

19. Southern *Loyalty*

A man from the deep South was about to jump from the window of a building, when a passer-by saw him and tried to talk him out of it. "For the sake of your mother, don't do it!" the passer-by pleaded.

"I don't have a mother," the would-be suicide said hopelessly.

"Well, think of your father."

"I don't have a father," the despondent man replied.

"Well, think of your wife!" the passer-by persisted.

"I never married," the dejected fellow said.

"Well then, think of Robert E. Lee!"

"Robert E. Lee! Who's he?"

"Never mind, Yankee. Go ahead and jump."

20. *Example*

"The new washerwoman has stolen two of our towels; the crook!" exclaimed the wife.

"Which towels, dear?" her husband asked.

"You know," she replied, "those we got from the hotel in Miami Beach."

21. *Fool* All The People

An exciting ball game was in progress, and the score was tied. The batter was up and the count was three balls and two strikes. The team, knowing the umpire was crooked, agreed for their pitcher to wind up and pretend to throw the ball. At the same time the catcher would hit his mitt, as if the ball had been thrown.

"Strike three," called the umpire, as the pitcher pretended to throw the ball.

In a rage the batter threw down his bat, "You dirty bum," he cried, "that ball was three feet outside!"

22. Only *Kidding*

A man-about-town was sitting in the barber's chair having a shave and manicure.

"You're cute," he said to the pretty young manicurist. "How about a date tonight?"

The manicurist smiled and said, "I'm sorry, but you see, I'm married."

"Big deal," said the man-about-town. "Phone the bum and tell him you'll be home late tonight."

"You tell him," said the manicurist sweetly. "He's shaving you."

23. Whereabouts Unknown

Fred Abernathy read the obituary column of the daily paper. All of Fred's friends knew of his habits, so one day they decided to play a trick on him by placing his name and picture in the obituaries.

The following morning Fred picked up his newspaper, turned to the obituary page, and there he saw his name, his biography and his photo.

Startled, he went to the telephone and rang up his pal, George. "Listen," he said. "Do you have the morning paper? You do? Please turn to the obituary page. You have? What do you see in the second column?"

There was a pause, then George said, "Holy smoke! It's you, Fred! It's you all right! Listen, where are you calling from?"

Parade

24. Asleep—Might Miss Out

A big executive boarded a New York to Chicago train. He explained to the porter: "I'm a heavy sleeper and I want you to be sure and wake me at 3:00 A.M. to get off in Buffalo. Regardless of what I say, get me up, for I have some important business there."

The next morning he awakened in Chicago. He found the porter, and really poured it on with abusive language.

After he had left, someone said, "How could you stand there and take that kind of talk from that man?"

The porter said: "That ain't nothing. You should have heard what the man said that I put off in Buffalo."

BIBLE

25. The Popular *Bible*

"Would you care to read the Bible and pray before retiring?" asked the hostess of a clerical delegate she was entertaining in her home.

Upon being assured he would be glad for the privilege, the lady said to her young son, "Bobby, go to the other room and bring that big book that mother and daddy read so much."

Soon Bobby returned with a Sears, Roebuck catalog.

> 400 *More Snappy Stories That Preachers Tell*
> —by Paul E. Holdcraft

26. *Blind* Leading Blind

Two lawyers were bosom friends. Much to the amazement of one of them, the other became a Sunday school teacher.

"Why," he protested, "I bet you don't even know the Lord's Prayer."

"Everybody knows that," the other replied. "It's 'Now I lay me down to sleep . . .' "

"You win," said the other admiringly, "I didn't know you knew so much about the Bible."

27. In Line of *Duty*

A driver tucked this note under the windshield wiper of his automobile: "I've circled the block for twenty minutes. I'm late for an appointment and if I don't park here I'll lose my job. 'Forgive us our trespasses.' "

When he came back he found a parking ticket and this note: "I've circled the block for twenty years and if I don't give you a ticket, I'll lose my job. 'Lead us not into temptation.' "

28. *Ignorance*

"Who will open the bidding on this antique bust of Chaucer?" asked the auctioneer.

"Sir," said an aristocratic lady among the bidders, "that is not 'Chaucer,' that is definitely, 'Boswell.' "

"Now that you mention it ma'am, I guess you're right," said the auctioneer. "I never did know too much about the Bible."

29. Scripture Knowledge

A traveling man one night found himself obliged to remain in a small town because of a washout on the railroad. He turned to the waitress with: "This certainly looks like the Flood."

"The what?"

"The Flood. You have read about the Flood, and the Ark landing on Mount Ararat, surely."

"No, mister," she replied, "I ain't seen a paper for three weeks."

A Bit of Honey

BOY—GIRL

30. *Sacrifice*

The young man poured out his heart's devotion on paper as he wrote to the girl of his dreams:

"Darling:

I would climb the highest mountain, swim the widest stream, cross the burning desert, die at the stake for you.

P.S. I will see you on Saturday—if it doesn't rain."

31. *Purposeful*

Two small sons and their father were watching a popular program on television, when the commercial came on the screen. This commercial showed two brothers in a high-speed motorboat. One of the boys was driving and had apparently not used this particular hair dressing. His hair was all tangled and unruly. His twin brother was in the back seat with his arm around a beautiful young lady. His hair was well-combed and apparently he had used this miracle preparation.

One of the boys watching the commercial said, "I'll tell you one thing; I'll never use that stuff on my hair."

"Why not?" asked his father.

The lad looked up at his dad and said, "Who wants to kiss a girl when you can drive?"

A Bit of Honey

BUSINESS—SELLING

32. Easy Payment *Plan*

"Just tell me one good reason why you can't buy a new car now," said the persistent automobile salesman.

"Well, I'll tell you, sir," replied the farmer. "I'm paying installments on the car I swapped for the car I traded in as part payment on the car I own now."

33. Can't Find *Words* To Express

A tailor decided to order a "gismo" that's used to press sleeves, called a "Tailor's goose." Sitting down to write his letter, he suddenly realized he needed two of them. So he wrote:

"Dear Sir: Please send me two Tailor's gooses."

But that didn't sound exactly right, so he tore it up and began all over again: "Dear Sir: Please send me two Tailor's geeses."

That didn't sound right either, so again he tore up his letter and wrote: "Dear Sir: Please send me one Tailor's Goose. P.S. Please send me another one too."

34. *Camouflage*

The manager of a restaurant called his waitresses together. "Girls," he began, "I want you all to look your best today. Greet every customer with a smile, put on a little extra make-up, and see to it that your hair is in place."

"What's up," asked one of the girls. "Bunch of big shots coming in today?"

"No," explained the manager, "the meat's tough today."

35. *Eye* For An Eye

Two merchants were in keen competition. One of them dreamed that an angel visited him.

"I will give you anything you want, up to a million

dollars," said the angel, "if you are willing for me to let your competitor have double. What is your wish?"

"Angel, I wish, I wish, I wish I was blind in *one eye!*"

36. Very Little *Hope*

A retail store owner wired a manufacturer for a consignment of goods and by return wire received the following message: "We can't ship your goods until you pay for the last consignment." The store owner wired back, "Cancel that new order. I can't wait that long!"

Parade

37. *Authority*

"Young man," exclaimed the customer haughtily, "I'd like to speak with someone with a little authority."

"I think I can help ma'am," the clerk replied, "for I have as little authority as anyone I know around here."

38. *Embarrassing* Moments

Entering a department store, a little old lady was startled when a band began to play and a dignified executive pinned an orchid on her dress and handed her a crisp hundred dollar bill. She was the store's millionth customer. Television cameras were focused on her and reporters began interviewing.

"Tell me," one asked, "just what did you come here for today?"

The lady hesitated for a minute, then answered, "I'm on my way to the Complaint Department."

39. *Attention* Please

A farmer bought a mule, and the fellow who sold him the animal warned him that the mule would work well, provided he would show a great deal of love and affection. The farmer took the mule home and showed it all the love and affection he could for one week.

In spite of all, however, the mule wouldn't budge. Disgusted, the farmer complained to the dealer that he either had to correct the situation or return his money.

The man went to the farm and saw immediately that the mule was very well taken care of and loved by the farmer.

He then picked up a two-by-four in the barn and whacked the mule over the head with it.

Horrified, the farmer screamed, "I thought you said I should show him affection."

Replied the dealer, "Sure, but you got to get his attention first."

Parade

40. In The Nick of *Time*

The proprietor of a store which had recently been burglarized met a friend on the street.

"I am sorry to hear about the robbery," the friend said. "Did you lose much?"

The storekeeper shrugged. "Some. But it would have been a lot worse if the burglar had broken in the night before."

"Why?" the friend asked.

"Well, you see," said the storekeeper, "just the day of the robbery I marked everything down twenty per cent."

41. *Valuable* Mule

A fellow was speeding down the road when he came across a large group of people blocking the highway.

"What's happened?" he asked someone in the group.

"It was an accident. A mule kicked my mother-in-law," he was told.

"But, why all the crowd. Are all these relatives?" he asked perplexedly.

The fellow replied, "No, it's an auction sale. These people are all trying to buy the mule."

42. *Beauty*

"I'd give five dollars for a lock of her hair," said the young man in love.

"Give me ten dollars and I'll get you the whole thing," said the pal. "I know where she bought it."

43. *Partnership*

A kidnaper took a man's wife and sent a note asking the man to leave fifty thousand dollars, or he'd never see his wife again.

When the kidnaper came for the money, he found a note

that said, "I'm not leaving you any money, but I am interested in your business."

44. *Enterprising*

On a trip through the hill country, a motorist stopped at a small crossroads store for a soft drink. The proprietor, who had been resting comfortably in a rocker on the front porch, got up and followed the customer inside. He said he had soft drinks in the quart size only, and that they were a dollar a bottle.

"But isn't that a little high?" asked the man.

"Well," replied the storekeeper, "I had to get up to wait on you."

"But you won't get many customers at that price, will you?"

The proprietor grinned, and said, "Won't need many."

45. *Dilemma*

The customer wanted to buy a chicken and the butcher had only one in stock. He weighed it and said, "A beauty. That will be $1.25, lady."

"Oh, that's not quite large enough," said the customer. The butcher put the chicken back in the refrigerator, rolled it around on the ice several times—then back on the scales again.

"This one is $1.85," he said, adding his thumb for good weight.

"Oh, that's fine!" said the customer. "I'll take both of them."

46. Hard *Sale*

Two shrewd business partners bought a special lot of suits. In the lot was a purple one, which they couldn't sell.

One of the partners became so angry about the purple suit, he went home. "I won't be back until you sell it," he said furiously, slamming the door behind him.

His partner called him at home in a couple of hours and said, "Come on back, I sold it."

Returning to the store and finding his partner scratched, cut and bleeding, he inquired, "What's the matter? Did you have to fight the customer to sell it?"

"No, but I had quite a time with his seeing-eye dog."

47. The *Advantages*

"This house," said the real estate salesman, "has both its good points and its bad points. To show you I'm honest, I'm going to tell you about both. The disadvantages are, that there is a chemical plant one block south and a slaughterhouse a block north."

"What are the advantages?" inquired the prospective buyer.

"The advantage is that you can always tell which way the wind is blowing."

48. A *Lady*

A dignified-looking, middle-aged gentleman decided to take advantage of a special sale and buy his wife a pair of nylons. After waiting about an hour on the fringe of a screaming, pushing mob of women, he plunged toward the counter with both arms flying. Suddenly a shrill voice hollered out, "Can't you act like a gentleman?"

"I've been acting like a gentleman for over an hour and it got me nowhere," he replied, still plowing toward the counter. "Now, I'm going to act like a lady!"

Parade

49. Taken *In*

The young convert worked as a clerk in a store operated on strictly Christian principles.

One day an elegant lady came in to buy some tapestry. Producing a roll from the lowest shelf, he said, "This is $1.98 a yard, madam."

"Young man, I can afford the very best and I want the very best," the prospective customer declared.

"Well, this is $2.98 a yard," said the clerk, producing the most expensive price range they had in fabrics.

"Young man, I don't think you understand—I want the very best!" the customer said emphatically.

The clerk reached for another roll of $2.98 quality material. "We have this one at $9.98 a yard," he said.

"Fine," responded the customer, "that's just what I want!"

The owner came into the store later and was told of the transaction.

"But how can you reconcile a deal such as that with Scripture?" he asked.

Scratching his head, the young man replied, "She was a stranger and I took her in."

50. *Economy*

The young couple walked into a car dealer's showroom and was taken back by the suggested price of a compact car. "But that's almost the cost of a big car," the husband said.

"Well," replied the salesman, "if you want economy, you've got to pay for it."

51. *Trust*

A Baptist Deacon had advertised a cow for sale.

"How much are you asking for it?" inquired a prospective purchaser.

"A hundred and fifty dollars," said the advertiser.

"And how much milk does she give?"

"Four gallons a day," he replied.

"But how do I know that she will actually give that amount?" asked the purchaser.

"Oh, you can trust me," reassured the advertiser, "I'm a Baptist Deacon."

"I'll buy it," replied the other. "I'll take the cow home and bring you back the money later. You can trust me, I'm a Presbyterian Elder."

When the Deacon arrived home he asked his wife, "What is a Presbyterian Elder?"

"Oh," she explained, "a Presbyterian Elder is about the same as a Baptist Deacon."

"Oh, dear," groaned the Deacon, "I have lost my cow!"

CHILDREN—HOME

52. *Grandchildren*

"Did I ever tell you about my grandchildren?" a proud grandfather asked his friend.

"No," replied the friend, "and you don't know how much I have appreciated it."

53. *Helpless*

The little boy said he was attending the wrong school. "I can't read and I can't write," he complained, "and they won't let me talk."

54. *Consideration*

After achieving great popularity, a renowned film star seemed despondent.

"I don't understand it," his agent protested. "You're in demand all over the world. You have plenty of money, and you have everything else you could possibly want."

"Bah!" snorted the actor. "What good is money to me? Here I am with everything in life a man could need, and my poor old mother has to starve in a garret."

Parade

55. *Bad Language*

A child was using bad language. So father and mother decided to wash out his mouth next time.

Father came home and was told by mother the child had used bad language again.

"Well, did you wash out his mouth?" asked dad.

"Yes," replied the mother, "but you should hear him now!"

56. *Truth* Will Come Out

A mother, father and son were dining in the town's swankiest restaurant. The father, having just closed a big business deal and feeling in an expensive mood, insisted on ordering the largest porterhouse steaks. The mother, a thrifty soul, summoned the waiter and said, "Please wrap what's left for the dog."

The boy, overhearing the conversation, leaped from his chair and squeaked, "Goody, goody, we're going to get a dog!"

Parade

57. *Support*

Grandfather was eighty-six when he took his first airplane ride. The plane circled around for about ten minutes, then landed.

"Well, Grandpa," he was asked, "how did you like your first ride?"

Rather shakily Grandpa answered, "Fine, but I never really put my weight on the blame thing."

58. *Going Along*

When the late King George the Sixth was a lad, he stood one winter morning with his older brother Edward, their noses pressed against a window of the palace, looking enviously at a group of cockney urchins playing snowball outside the palace.

Finally, the temptation became too great for them, and seeing an opportunity, as the governess left the room, they put on hats and coats and slipped outside to join the happy group.

Soon a badly aimed snowball, smashing right through the window of the palace, brought the palace guard running "on the double." In no time at all the sheepish group of youngsters was ushered into the presence of the precinct sergeant.

"What's your name, boy," the sergeant asked the first in line.

"My name is Edward, Prince of Wales," said the boy, standing haughtily at attention.

"A smart guy, eh?" said the sergeant. "And what's your name?" he asked the second in line.

"My name is Albert, Duke of Windsor," said the second lad.

By this time the sergeant was furious. "I've never seen such a bunch of liars in all my life," he exploded.

"And, what's your name?" he asked the next little fellow.

The little boy hesitated a moment, then wiping his nose on his sleeve, he replied: "I'm going to stand wiv' my buddies, guvnor ... I'm the Archbishop of Canterbury."

59. Understanding The *Problem*

A mother, visiting a department store, took her son to the toy department. Spying a gigantic rocking horse he climbed upon it and rocked back and forth for almost an hour.

"Come on, son," the mother pleaded. "I have to get home to get father's dinner."

The little lad refused to budge and all her efforts were unavailing. The department manager also tried to coax the little fellow, without meeting with any success. Eventually, in desperation they called for the store's psychiatrist. Gently he walked over and whispered a few words in the boy's ear, and immediately the lad jumped off and ran to his mother's side.

"How did you do it?" the mother asked incredibly. "What did you say to him?"

The psychiatrist hesitated for a moment, then said: "All I said was, 'If you don't jump off that rocking horse at once, son, I'll knock the stuffing out of you!' "

60. First *Steps*

Mother had made the mistake of leaving baby in her husband's care while she went out into the back yard to hang out the washing. Father buried himself behind a newspaper, and forgot all about the baby until he heard a series of thumps, and a frightful wail.

"Martha," called the father excitedly, running to the back door, "Come quick! Junior just took his first twenty-three steps!"

61. God's Little *Angel*

A little boy in Aberdeen, Scotland, was disciplined by his mother, who used to say to him when he was naughty, "Now, God won't like that." And when he was particularly unruly or disobedient, she would say, "God will be angry."

Usually these admonitions were sufficient, but one night when she had prunes for his dessert at supper, he rebelled. He refused to finish the prunes on his plate. She pleaded. She coaxed. Finally, she said, "Now, God won't like this. God doesn't like little boys who refuse to finish all their prunes."

But the little fellow was quite unmoved. She went further to say, "God will be angry." But for some reason or other the little boy stubbornly refused to take the last two prunes which lay on his plate ... dark blue, wrinkled tokens of his rebellion.

"Well," said the mother, "you must now go to bed. You have been a very naughty boy, and God is angry."

So she packed him upstairs and put him to bed. No sooner had she come down, than a violent thunderstorm broke out. The lightning was more vivid than usual. The thunder clumped up and down the sky with shattering reverberations. The suddenly angry wind threw handfuls of rain against the windows. It was a most violent storm, and she thought her little son would be terrified, and that she should go up and comfort him. Quietly she opened his bedroom door, expecting to find him whimpering in fear, perhaps with the covers pulled over his head. But to her surprise, he was not in bed at all, but had gone over to the window. With his face pressed against the window pane, she heard him mutter, "My, my, sic a fuss to mak' ower twa prunes."

A Man Called Peter

62. No Place Like *Home*

An out-of-town salesman went into a restaurant and asked the waitress to fry him two eggs so hard the edges would be black, two slices of burnt toast, and a cup of cold coffee. "Then sit down and nag me," he pleaded. "I'm homesick."

63. Inherited

Mother was helping Sonny with his homework, and asked, "How much is five and five?"

"Twelve," said the son.

"Not bad for a little shaver," said his dad, who was listening. "He only missed it by two."

64. Can't *Hide*

A little boy took some cookies from the cookie jar without permission, and his mother caught him.

She asked, "Son, don't you know God saw you take those cookies?"

"Yes," replied the boy, "but He didn't see me eat them. I ate them under the table."

65. Setting The *Example*

During a blistering hot day, a family was entertaining

guests for dinner. When all were seated, the man of the house turned to his six-year-old son and asked him to say the blessing.

"But daddy, I don't know what to say," he protested.

"Oh, just say what you've heard me say," the mother chimed in.

Obediently, he bowed his little head and said, "Oh, Lord, why did I invite these people here on a hot day like this!"

66. Missing the Mark

Jimmy's mother, a believer in the "be-a-little-gentleman-and-don't fight" school of upbringing was trying to instill this noble outlook into her pugnacious young son.

"Jimmy, when that naughty boy threw stones at you, why didn't you come and tell me instead of throwing them back?"

"What good would that do?" snorted Jimmy. "You can't hit the broad side of a barn."

67. Enlightenment

The five-year-old was busily drawing, and his mother inquired what it was.

"I'm drawing a picture of Adam and Eve," said the boy.

"But, nobody knows what Adam and Eve looked like," said the mother.

"They will," replied the boy, "when I get through with them."

Parade

68. Well Versed

Two little boys were bragging about the abilities of their mothers.

"I'll bet my mama can talk one hour on any subject," said one little boy.

"Huh!" replied the other little fellow proudly, "My mama can talk one hour without a subject."

69. Fact or Fiction

The pastor had just been telling his visiting grandchildren a fascinating bedtime story.

The little ones listened to him breathlessly, but when the tale was finally ended, Johnny took a deep breath and asked, "Grandpa, was that a true story or were you just preaching?"

70. Harmful *Deductions*

The Temperance lecturer was illustrating the evils of liquor. Dramatically producing two glasses, one filled with water and the other filled with whiskey, he proceeded to drop a live worm into each glass. The worm in the water swam around in a lively manner, while the one in the whiskey promptly curled up and died.

"Now then," he exclaimed triumphantly, "what does this prove?"

"If you drink whiskey you won't have worms."

71. *Fear*

Little girl to her boastful daddy: "Aren't you afraid of bears, or snakes, or lightning, or mice, daddy?"

"Of course not."

"Aren't you really, truly 'fraid of anything, daddy, but just mama?"

72. Modern *Discipline*

Parents nowadays are too busy even to punish their kids! Mothers are running to bingo games. Fathers are running off to golf courses and bowling alleys. Before they leave the house they just say: "Son, we left a strap on the bed. If you do something wrong, hit yourself six times."

73. *Brotherly* Regard

Tom: "How would you teach a girl to swim?"
Bill: "That's easy. Take her little hand in yours, lead her gently down to the water, and say, 'Now, don't be afraid, my dear. I wouldn't let anything hurt you.'"
Tom: "But, she's my sister."
Bill: "Oh, just push her off the dock."

74. *Generally Speaking*

"Daddy, said the little girl as she watched her father, a minister, struggle with his next Sunday's sermon, "doesn't God tell you what to say?"

"Of course, He does, honey," the father beamed.

"Then why do you keep scratching out some of the words?"

75. Bad *Intentions*

A rather small boy was frightened of the large bulldog that occupied the yard next to his home.

One day, feeling rather adventurous, the little boy climbed the fence and the huge bulldog rushed up to him and licked his face. The boy began to scream and his mother arrived on the scene almost immediately.

"Did he bite you, darling?"

"No," whimpered the little boy, "but he tasted me."

76. Great *Sacrifice*

A group of youngsters were caught with the evidence on them. All, with the exception of one little boy, had sticky faces from the candy they had taken.

The policeman asked him, "How come you're not eating any? Didn't you help steal it?"

"Yes," said the little boy. "I helped steal it but I didn't eat any of it. I gave mine up for Lent."

77. *Exasperation*

Little Johnny was having himself a terrific time on his first plane trip. He pushed every button in sight, ran through the aisles at top speed and finally crashed into the stewardess as she was serving a tray of coffee.

The stewardess picked herself up and grabbed young Johnny by the arm. "Son," she cooed sweetly, "why don't you go outside and play?"

78. *Cause* and Effect

Mother: "Willie, why did you kick your little brother in the stomach?"

Willie: "He turned around."

CHURCH—BELIEVERS

79. *Economy*

A church convention of over a thousand delegates met for a week in a certain city.

"I suppose business is good, with all these delegates here," a regular customer asked one of the storekeepers.

Lamented the storekeeper: "They came with the Ten Commandments in one hand, a ten dollar bill in the other hand, and they haven't broken either of them yet."

80. *Skepticism*

A little boy, after attending Sunday school, was asked by his mother what he learned.

"We heard about a man named Moses. He went behind the lines and rescued the Israelites. Then he came to the Red Sea, and called his engineers and they built a pontoon bridge. After they got across, he saw the enemy tanks approaching, so he got on his walkie-talkie and called headquarters, and they sent the dive dombers and blew up the bridge. Then the Israelites rode on."

"Now, son, it wasn't like that at all was it?"

"Well, not exactly. But, if I told you how the teacher said it really happened, you wouldn't have believed it either!"

81. Dislike *Change*

The Baptist and Christian churches were trying to merge. All the members of both churches agreed, except one old-timer.

"No," he said, as he shook his head.

"Why, sir?" he was asked.

"Well, my mother and father were Baptists, my grandparents were Baptists, all of my people were Baptists . . . and nobody is going to make a Christian out of me now!"

82. Long-face *Religion*

A very young niece was visiting a holier-than-thou aunt in the country for the summer. Her puritanical attitude was in constant evidence. Every time the little niece wanted to do something, the long-faced aunt would say, "Don't do that . . . you can't do that."

One day the little niece was walking down the road, very unhappy, when she came upon a long-faced mule near the fence. She walked over, patted its head, and said, "Don't feel bad, Mr. Mule, my aunt has religion too."

83. *Limited* Membership

Oil was found on the property of a small church of forty members. As the money began to roll in, they called a special meeting to decide what to do with the money.

Deacon Brown said, "I move we divide this money among the forty members—and further, I move that no new members be taken in."

84. Wrong Church—Right *Pew*

A woman who "enjoyed her religion" visited a very staid and formal church.

"Amen!" she said, as the preacher brought out a point with which she agreed.

"Madam," said the usher standing nearby, "Please try and restrain yourself. We don't allow that in this church."

In a few moments she was so carried away by the sermon that she shouted, "Amen, Praise the Lord, Hallelujah!"

The usher rushed to her side: "Madam! You must quiet down immediately or leave!"

"I didn't mean to disturb the service . . . but I am just so happy since I found the Lord," she explained.

"You may have found the Lord," retorted the usher severely, "but I am quite sure you didn't find Him here!"

85. Real *Sacrifice*

Sonny, after hearing a Lenten sermon, decided to give up something for this special Lenten season.

"Son," his mother said, "it should be something that you are fond of."

"Well, ma," replied the lad, with fingers crossed, "I'm giving up Sunday school, 'cause I like that better than anything else."

86. *Quiet* Please

A little boy was playing with his blocks when his father entered the room.

"Quiet, Dad, I'm building a church."

The father, thinking that he would test his son along the lines of religious knowledge, said, "Why do we want to be quiet in church?"

"We have to, because the people are sleeping."

87. Choosing *Sides*

A man was going to attend a Hallowe'en party dressed in the costume of the devil. On his way it began to rain, so he darted into a church where a revival meeting was in progress.

At the sight of his devil's costume, people began to scatter through the doors and windows.

One lady got her coat sleeve caught on the arm of one of the seats and as the man came closer she pleaded, "Satan, I've been a member of this church for twenty years, but I've really been on your side all the time."

88. Divine *Nudges*

A pastor called a congregational meeting to decide whether to repair the church building or tear it down and build a new one. Most of the brethren wanted the new church, but the decision seemed to rest upon the attitude and generosity of a wealthy deacon. When called upon to express himself, the brother arose and said: "It is true the old church is badly in need of repairs, but I think we should do that instead of building a new one. I'll subscribe fifty dollars toward repairing the old church."

Being a portly man, as he took his seat, he jarred the building, and a piece of loose plaster fell on his head. Jumping to his feet he said: "This building is in worse shape than I thought. I'll make it five hundred for repairs."

As he took his seat again, another member was heard to mutter a prayer: "Oh, Lord, hit him again!"

400 More Snappy Stories That Preachers Tell

89. Ultra *Conservatism*

A certain congregation was about to erect a new church edifice. The building committee, in consecutive meetings, passed the following resolutions: (1) We shall build a new church. (2) The new building is to be located on the site of the old one. (3) The material in the old building is to be used in the new one. (4) We shall continue to use the old building until the new one is completed.

400 More Snappy Stories That Preachers Tell

90. *Unity*

The passer-by noticed the different songs in the nearby

churches. He jokingly exclaimed, "There's real unity among the brethren."

Baptist Church was singing, "Will There Be Any Stars in My Crown?"

Methodist Church was singing, "No, Not One."

Presbyterian Church was singing, "Oh, That Will be Glory for Me."

91. Baptist *Origin*

"Some people say that the Baptist denomination started with John the Baptist, but it was much earlier than that," said a great Baptist leader as he spoke to a large gathering of Baptist ministers. "In fact, it started way over in the Old Testament. In the 13th chapter of Genesis, it says Lot said to Abraham: 'You go your way and I'll go mine.' That's when the Baptists began."

92. *Blushes*

A group of women was talking together. One lady said, "Our congregation is sometimes down to thirty and forty on Sunday night."

Another said, "That's nothing, sometimes our group is down to six or seven."

An old maid added her bit, "It's so bad in our church on Sunday night that when the minister says, 'Dearly beloved,' it makes me blush."

93. *Willingness*

During the holiday season an enthusiastic Salvation Army lass was going from door to door with a collection box. She went to the door of one old lady and asked if she would like to help the carolers.

"I'd love to, dearie," replied the old lady, "but I've got bronchitis something terrible this year, and I couldn't sing a note."

94. Collection *Inspection*

This new collection box has some new features. When you drop in a quarter or more it doesn't make a sound! Drop in a dime and it tinkles like a bell; a nickel blows a whistle, and a penny fires a shot; and when you don't drop anything in, the box takes your picture.

F'r Instance

95. *Jumping at Conclusions*

Several churches in the South decided to hold union services. The leader was a Southern Baptist and proud of his denomination.

"How many Southern Baptists are here?" he asked on the first night of the revival.

All except one little old lady raised their hands.

"Lady, what are you?" asked the leader.

"I'm a Methodist," meekly replied the lady.

"Why are you a Methodist?" persisted the leader.

"Well," replied the little old lady, "my grandparents were Methodists, my mother was a Methodist, my late husband was a Methodist."

"Well," retorted the leader, "just supposing all your relatives had been morons, what would that have made you?"

"Oh! I see. A Southern Baptist, I suppose," the lady replied meekly.

96. Stopping *Competition*

A Baptist family had a death in the family while their minister was out of town.

They asked the local Methodist minister to conduct the funeral service. He said he would have to check with the Bishop. He wired the Bishop, "Could I bury a Baptist?"

The Bishop wired back: "Sure, bury all the Baptists you can!"

97. In *Neutral*

There was a church with a reputation for being very hard on janitors, never being able to keep one. After one old man had been there for several years, someone asked him, "How in the world do you manage to get along in this church with so many contrary orders and instructions?"

The old man just smiled sweetly and said, "I just puts my mind in neutral and let them push me around."

F'r Instance

98. *Reservation*

A notorious gambler came to the altar during a revival meeting. After the meeting the minister told him to bring all of his gambling equipment to the next meeting and build a fire with them.

"You'll have to excuse me, preacher, but I just can't do that."

"Why not?" inquired the minister. "You've been converted, haven't you?"

"Sure, I'm converted," said the gambler, "but that don't make me foolish. Suppose I throw all that stuff away and then I backslide; that would leave me in a fine predicament, wouldn't it?"

F'r Instance

99. Take Your *Choice*

A new convert was put to work ushering and taking up the offering, and was very enthusiastic in his duties. One day, while taking up the offering, he stopped in front of the town's old miser, who was known never to put anything in the plate. This man paid no attention to him, but the young fellow remained standing, with the plate under the miser's nose.

Some of the other ushers tried to signal him to move on, but he continued to stand there.

Finally, in a clear voice that carried around the church, he said, "Ain't you goin' to put anything in the offering?"

"No," answered the miser gruffly.

"Well, then," said the usher "take some out. It's for the heathen."

F'r Instance

100. *Exemption* Claimed

A little boy attended church for the first time. And as the offering plate was passed, he said, very brightly, "Daddy, you don't have to pay for me. I'm under six."

101. *Long-Winded*

Right in the middle of the service, and just before the sermon, one of the congregation remembered she had forgotten to turn off the gas under the roast. Hurriedly she scribbled a note and passed it to the usher to give to her husband. Unfortunately, the usher misunderstood her intention and took it to the pulpit. Unfolding the note, the preacher read aloud: "Please go home and turn off the gas."

102. Don't *Sleep* In Church

A parishioner had dozed off to sleep during the morning service.

"Will all who want to go to heaven stand?" the preacher asked.

All stood, except the sleeping parishioner.

"Well, will all who want to go to the other place stand?" asked the preacher.

At that moment someone suddenly dropped a songbook. Quickly the sleeping man jumped to his feet and stood sheepishly facing the preacher.

He mumbled confusedly, "Well, preacher, I don't know what we're voting for, but it looks like you and I are the only ones for it."

103. Just *Checking*

A Sunday school teacher was explaining the Day of Judgment.. "Thunder will boom," he told the pupils. "Flames will pour from the heavens. There will be gigantic floods, and earthquakes will split open the ground to swallow all."

"Will I get off from school?" interrupted a little girl.

104. *Lost*

A little boy asked his Sunday school teacher the question, "Where did I come from?"

"Dust," the teacher replied.

"Where am I going," he asked.

"Dust," the teacher replied.

One day, later, the little boy called to his mama, "Mama, come upstairs quick. Somebody is under my bed, either coming or going."

105. *Curiosity*

An Orthodox Jew was in a store where they sold ham. Just as he inquired the price of one of them it began to thunder.

Raising his eyes toward heaven, he said, "Well, Lord, can't I even ask the price?"

106. A *Helping* Hand

A Salvation Army lassie was doing personal work one day when she asked a man if he was saved.

The man said, "Young lady, I will have you know I'm an Episcopalian Bishop!"

The young lady, looking up in his face, very sweetly replied, "Sir, there's hope for the vilest."

107. *Temptation* Too Great

Pat's conscience was battling with his appetite one Friday, when he saw the man at the next table dig into a thick, juicy steak.

"Give me a whale sandwich on rye bread, with French Fries," he told the waitress.

"Whale? That's not on the menu, sir."

"Then bring me a thick sirloin," said Pat condescendingly. "The Lord knows I tried."

108. Need *Change*

Two southern mountaineers were talking. One said, "I hear they have a new pope in Rome."

"Yes," said the other. "And I think they should have a Southern Baptist this time. Them Catholics have been in long enough."

109. *Indirect* Revenge

A Quaker became exasperated with his cow for kicking over a pail of milk.

He warned: "Thou knowest that, because of my religion, I can't punish thee. But if thee doeth that again, I will sell thee to a Baptist preacher and he will kick thee so thee won't be able to kick it over again."

110. *Safety*

The father was a Christian Scientist and always carried a copy of Mrs. Eddy's works in his pocket. Accompanied by his little son, he had an occasion to cross a lot where a good-sized goat was feeding. As they approached the goat the boy showed fear, whereat his father told him to think it not possible for the animal to harm them; but the boy, remembering previous encounters with the goat, in which he came out second best, did not grow any braver.

"Papa, you're a Christian Scientist, all right," he said, "and so am I; but the goat doesn't know it."

111. *Spelling*

At a church meeting everyone was asked to write down their denomination.

One man wrote Baptist.

"I thought you were a Presbyterian," said one.

"I am, but I didn't know how to spell Presbyterian."

"Well, why didn't you just write a 'P.' "

"I thought about it, but I was afraid everybody would think I was *Piscopalian*."

112. Complete *Coverage*

A Methodist visited a city right at the time of a large Baptist Convention.

"My, this is remarkable!" he exclaimed. "I've never seen so many Baptists in all my life before."

"Oh, that's nothing," replied another out-of-town visitor. "In our state, even the Warden of the penitentiary is a Baptist, as well as over half of the inmates."

113. Good *Habit*

"Won't I look pretty at Sunday school in this?" said a little boy to his mother, just after the mother had bought him a new suit.

"Oh, do you go to Sunday school?" asked the clerk, as he wrapped the suit.

"Sure," replied the lad, "where else is there to go on Sunday?"

114. Strictly *Confidential*

One day an old mountain deacon was caught in the alley, taking a little drink.

A fellow deacon said, "You know you ought not to do tnat . . . you know the Lord will see you."

"Yes, Brother Deacon, but He ain't a big blabbermouth like a lot of people I know."

115. *Example*

A man came home and seeing his children on the front steps, asked what they were doing.

"We're playing church," they answered.

It didn't resemble a church service, as they were standing and talking.

The puzzled father inquired further and was told, "Well, we've already sung, prayed and preached, and now we're outside on the steps smoking."

116. *Predicament*

The most terrible feeling I have ever had, is to be caught in church with only a $20 bill.

CLERGYMEN

117. Model *Preacher*

The young preacher was flattered when someone described him as a "model" preacher.

His pride, however, soon vanished when he turned to his dictionary and found the definition of Model: "A small imitation of the real thing."

He was a little more cautious the next time. On being described as a "warm" preacher, he turned to his pocket dictionary, which read, "Warm . . . Not so hot."

118. Team Work

Two workmen, Jewish and Catholic, were making road repairs when a rabbi came by and was observed by both of them entering a saloon.

"Isn't that a shame!" exclaimed the Catholic workman. "A man of the cloth has no business to be going into a saloon. He should be at church or visiting the sick in the hospital."

At that moment a priest entered the same saloon.

The Catholic workman said, "There must be somebody pretty sick in there."

119. *Tenacity*

There was a certain energetic young preacher who had a thriving country church. He was always prodding his people on to do greater things for God. He spent much time in preparation of his sermons. There was a certain deacon in his congregation who did little and seemed to care less. It caused the young preacher much concern. On several occasions the preacher would tell him exactly what he thought. The old deacon never caught the point. The old deacon always thought he was referring to someone else. One Sunday the preacher made it plain as to whom he was talking. Following the service the deacon said, "Preacher, you sure told them today."

The next sermon was still more pointed than ever. Again the deacon said, "Preacher, you sure told them today."

The next Sunday it rained so hard that no one was at the church except this one deacon. The preacher thought that he would now know about whom he was talking. The sermon went straight to the deacon who was the only one in the congregation. Following the service, the deacon walked up to the preacher and said, "Preacher, you sure told them if they had been here."

A Bit of Honey

120. *Strategist*

A Southern preacher got up one Sunday morning and said, "There is twelve chicken thieves in this congregation this mawnin'—including Brother Johnson." Brother Johnson did not like it very much, naturally. After the service he called on the preacher and told him that he should not bawl him out in public that way, and that he would have to take it back and apologize in the evening service. The preacher promised to do so. At the evening service he said, "Brethren, at this mawnin's service I said there was twelve chicken thieves in the congregation, including Brother Johnson, but I want to take that statement back and apologize to Brother Johnson. I say now there were eleven chicken thieves in this congregation this mawnin', not counting Brother Johnson."

A Bit of Honey

121. *Cooperation*

A member of the Catholic Church approached her priest, and said, "Father, my dog died, and I want to know if you think it is all right to have a funeral for him."

The priest said, "Yes, I think it's all right, if you desire one."

"And who do you think would be a minister to conduct it?"

The priest wasn't too happy with the thoughts of this funeral, so he said, "I know a good Presbyterian minister down the street, I believe he will conduct it for you."

"Oh, thank you, Father, and just one more question, How much do you think I should pay him for it, $200 or $300?"

The priest's eyes lit up, and as he slipped his arm around his parishioner, he said, "Why, my friend, why didn't you say it was a Catholic dog?"

122. *Attention*

"What did the preacher preach about?" the little boy was asked after church.

"He didn't say," he replied.

123. *Volume Preaching*

A hundred years or so ago there was a clergyman in Scotland who had so tremendous a voice that he was locally known as Roarin' Harry. Unhappily, his preaching was in no way powerful as his voice. Once he promised to take a service at a nearby church on the following Sunday, and the fact was announced by the preacher he was to relieve, who, after giving his name, added drily, "Concerning whom it may be truly said that, though we have sometimes heard a better preacher, we have never heard a preacher better."

124. *Empty Speaker*

A minister visited a rural family for dinner and they ate just before church.

He explained that he couldn't eat very much and preach a good message.

After dinner the wife asked the husband to go on to the service with the minister while she washed the dishes.

After the husband returned, she asked him how the message was.

"Oh, to tell you the truth," was the reply, "he may as well et."

125. *Convenience*

The Catholic priest was trying to get a Jew converted to his faith.

He said, "All you have to do is say three times, 'I was a Jew . . . now I'm a Catholic.'"

He said it, but the priest thought he had better check up on his convert one Friday at his home.

The Jew was frying chicken. "Now, you know you can't eat that chicken on Friday."

"Oh, yes, I can," he replied. "I dipped it in a pan three times and said, 'Once I was a chicken, now I am a fish.'"

126. *Enthusiastic* About Matter

A minister went hunting up in the mountains. Suddenly a big bear got after him. He took off so fast you could play checkers on his coat tail, but he couldn't find any place to hide.

Suddenly he saw a tree—but the lowest limb was twenty feet from the ground. He made a frantic leap for it, but missed it . . . however, he grabbed it on the way down.

127. Line of Least *Resistance*

The church member was delinquent in paying his pledge, and the matter was referred to the minister.

"You are a respectable citizen," the minister chided. "You always pay your debts to everyone else. Why not pay your debts to the Lord?"

"Well, to tell you the truth," the member answered, "He just doesn't push as hard as some of the others."

128. Appreciate Your *Loyalty*

A little old lady got into an argument with her pastor. The pastor thought he would never see her again. However, she showed up for the evening service the same Sunday.

"I thought you'd gone for good," he said to her.

"Pastor," she said, "I'm going to be loyal to my church, even if the devil is in the pulpit."

129. *Bored*

After a long, dry sermon the minister announced that he

wished to meet with the Board following the close of the service. The first man to arrive was a stranger. "You misunderstood my announcement. This is a meeting of the Board," said the minister.

"I know," said the man, "but if there is anyone here more bored than I am, I'd like to meet him."

130. Self *Justification*

The new minister was very strict about "keeping the Sabbath." After the morning service he called one of the deacons into the study.

"Deacon Jones," he said, "I heard you went to the ballgame last Sunday, instead of coming to church."

"That's a lie!" the deacon cried, "and what's more, I still have one of the fish to prove it!"

131. Wrong *Notes*

A minister who had a faulty memory was accustomed to writing notes on a card and inserting it in his inside coat pocket. When he forgot what he was to say, he would pull his coat back and refresh his memory with a quick glance.

One day he was preaching about the three Jewish boys, named (looking at the card) "Meshach, Shadrach and Abednego." As he continued, he said, "and they walked through the fiery furnace . . . these three Jewish boys named . . ." But the card had slipped down and he couldn't see the names. So he started over.

"So they walked through the fiery furnace . . . these three Jewish boys named . . ." he threw his coat back again, looked at the pocket, and said, "Hart, Shaffner and Marx."

132. Pretty *Wives*

A minister married a couple. The woman had on a veil and he could not see her face. After the ceremony the man asked the minister, "How much do I owe you?"

"No charge," replied the minister.

"But I want to show my appreciation," so the man gave him fifty cents.

About that time the bride pulled off her veil, and the minister, looking at the bride, gave the man twenty-five cents change.

133. In All *Tongues*

This real "hep" kid attended the morning service of a very dignified church. He was met by the pastor as he greeted the people after the conclusion of the service. The "hep" kid grabbed the minister's hand and said, "Dad, I really 'dig' that sermon."

The pastor was horrified and said, "Young man, I don't understand."

"Dad, I really 'went' for that sermon ... it really came down the middle ... loud and clear ... it was cool ... it was gone, man," answered the beatnik.

The pastor was really "shaken" at such jargon, and said, "Son, I just don't comprehend what you are saying."

"Well, dad, what I mean is, I really went for what you had to say, so much that I put twenty smackerooes in the collection plate."

All of a sudden the preacher's face lit up like a neon sign, and he said, with real understanding, "Crazy, man, crazy!"

134. Too *Costly*

A country preacher was preaching very pointedly to his congregation one Sunday night.

He said, "Now let the church walk."

Deacon Jones said, "Amen, let it walk."

The preacher then said, "Let the church run."

Deacon Jones said, "Amen, parson, let it run."

"Let the church fly," said the preacher.

"Amen, brother, let it fly," said Deacon Jones.

"Now it's going to take money to let it fly, brother."

"Let it walk," said Deacon Jones. "Let it walk."

135. Tired *Pushing*

The small town preacher rushed to the railroad station every day to watch the train go by. Members of his congregation thought his pastime juvenile and asked him to give it up.

"No, gentlemen," said he firmly. "I preach your sermons, teach your Sunday school, bury your dead, marry your young people, run your charities, and am chairman of every drive it pleases you to conduct. I won't give it up-seeing the train every day. I love it. It's the only thing that passes through this town that I don't have to push."

136. Two of A *Kind*

The train robber went from car to car, holding up the passengers and taking their money and jewelry.

Eventually he came to the last man, who said, "You wouldn't rob a preacher, would you?"

"What kind of a preacher are you?" the robber asked.

"I'm a Baptist."

The robber took the gun in his left hand, held out his right hand, and said, "Put it there, brother, I'm one, too."

137. Water *Power*

The new preacher, at his first service, had a pitcher of water and a glass on the pulpit. As he preached he drank, until the pitcher of water was completely gone.

After the service someone asked an old woman of the church, "How did you like the new pastor?"

"Fine," she said, "But he's the first windmill I ever saw that was run by water."

138. *Courtesy*

There was a long-winded preacher who preached from Genesis to Revelation in every sermon.

One day, after having practically covered the whole Bible, he said, "Now we have come to Isaiah—what will we do with him?"

One old man said, "He can have my seat brother, I'm leaving."

139. *Light* On Subject

During a business meeting in a small southern mountain church, one of the deacons said, "Pastor, I think we need a chandelier for the church."

"No," replied another deacon. "I'm against it."

"Why don't you think we need a chandelier, Brother Deacon?" asked the pastor.

"Well, first, nobody in the church can spell it; second, nobody in the church can play it; and third, what this church needs above all else, is mo' light!"

140. *Procrastination*

A minister was preaching and in his sermon said: "Who wants to go to heaven?"

Everybody held up their hands except one young boy.

"Son, don't you want to go to heaven when you die?"

"Yes, sir, when I die, but I thought you was getting up a load to go now."

141. Strange *Language*

A farmer drove his team of mules into town and was very late returning home.

"What took you so long?" asked his wife.

"Well," the farmer explained, "on the way I had to pick up the preacher, and from there on, them mules of ours didn't understand one word I said."

142. The Real *Need*

A couple was touring the Capitol in Washington, and the guide pointed to a tall, benevolent gentleman, as the congressional chaplain.

The lady asked, "What does the Chaplain do? Does he pray for the Senate or House?"

The guide answered, "No, he gets up—looks at the Congress, then prays for the country."

Parade

143. Good *Audience*

A preacher visited a family where the father had just died. He asked the young son, "What were your father's last words?"

"He didn't have any," said the boy. "Mama was with him to the end."

144. Hidden *Expense*

"How can you preach upon the subject 'Salvation is free,' and then take up a collection?" the pastor was asked.

"Well," replied the pastor, "It's like this. Suppose you lived on a mountain and there was a stream of crystal water nearby, and you wanted it piped in to your house. The water would be absolutely free, but you would still have to pay for the pipes."

145. Under *Pressure*

He was seriously ill and called for the pastor. "Pastor, if you pray for me to recover and I do, I will give you twenty-five thousand dollars toward the new church you are building."

The pastor prayed and the man got well. Although the pastor tried tactfully to remind him of his pledge, it met with no success. Finally, he frankly told him: "You promised to give twenty-five thousand dollars for the new church . . ."

"Did I?" said the recovered man. "Well, that should give you some idea of how sick I really was."

146. *Results*

On one of his pastoral visits a minister noticed two holes cut in a door and inquired what they were for.

"We have two cats, and that's for them to go out through," the man of the house explained.

"Well, why do you need two holes? Can't they both go out through the same hole?" questioned the minister.

"Friend," said the fellow, "when my wife says 'scat,' she means it!"

147. *Long-winded*

A Protestant college student invited his Catholic chum to attend church with him one Sunday.

The Catholic boy was most interested in the Protestant order of service and asked many questions.

When the preacher stepped into the pulpit to preach, removed his watch from his pocket and placed it on the pulpit, he asked, "What does it mean?"

The Protestant boy whispered, "It doesn't mean a thing."

148. Church *Attendance*

An old man never attended church. One day the church got on fire, and there, with everyone else, was the old man throwing water. After the fire had been extinguished, the minister said, "This is the first time I've seen you at church."

The old man replied, "And this is the first time I have ever seen this church on fire."

149. Pastoral *Calls*

Mother was busy upstairs and asked her little son to call her when the butcher came.

Shortly afterward the minister came calling.

"Mama, a man's here," the lad called to his mother.

The mother called back loudly, "Give him twenty-five cents out of my purse, and tell him I didn't like his tongue last week."

150. *Vindication*

In a certain town a report went the rounds that a local pastor had gone to a place where his wife was attending a meeting against his will, and had dragged her from the place and forced her to go home.

Upon learning of the gossip the minister inserted an item in the local paper as follows:

"In the first place I never attempted to influence my wife in her views of her choice of a meeting."

"In the second place my wife did not attend the meeting in question."

"In the third place, I did not attend the meeting."

"In the fourth place, neither my wife nor myself had any inclination to go to the meeting."

"Finally, I do not now have, and never had a wife."

400 More Snappy Stories That Preachers Tell

151. *Warning*

As the minister took the offering he said, "Some ministers feed the sheep, some lead the sheep, but now I'm going to shear the sheep."

152. *Candor*

A minister asked the little girl what she thought of her first church service.

"The music was nice," she said, "but the commercial was too long."

153. *Home* at Last

He had been around from church to church, trying to find a congenial congregation. Finally he stopped in a little church just as the congregation read with the minister:

"We have left undone those things which we ought to have done."

The man dropped into a pew with a sigh of relief. "Thank goodness," he observed, "I've found my crowd at last."

F'r Instance

154. *High Wages*

The three sons of a lawyer, a doctor and a minister, respectively, were talking about how much money their fathers made.

The lawyer's son said, "My father goes into court on a case and often comes home with as much as fifteen hundred dollars."

The doctor's son said, "My father performs an operation and earns as much as two thousand dollars for it."

The minister's son, determined not to be outdone, said, "That's nothing. My father preaches for just fifteen minutes on Sunday morning and it takes four men to carry the money."

155. *Disturbance*

Two ministers were talking. One said, "I would like to relocate my church. The Pennsylvania railroad runs right beside my church and every Sunday about the middle of the service, the train comes by and disturbs the service."

The other minister replied, "That's nothing. Every Sunday the Nickel-plate comes right down the middle of my aisles."

156. *Discharged*

Two friends were discussing their churches one day. One said, "By the way, we are firing our pastor."

"Why?" the friend asked.

"For two reasons," the other replied. "First, he has a poor delivery, and second, he has nothing to deliver."

157. Calling the *Signals*

The organist wanted to make an impression on the visiting clergyman with her musical accomplishment. She wrote a note to the old sexton who had been a little slack in his work of pumping enough air for the organ, and handed it to him just before the service started. But, making a natural mistake, the sexton passed the note on to the visiting clegyman, who opened it and read: *"Keep blowing away until I give the signal to stop."*

158. Questionable *Companionship*

An elderly lady had a parrot that was using offensive language. Every time the lady would come into the room it would say, "I wish she was dead. I wish she was dead."

She told her pastor about it and he said, "I have a parrot, too, but it is never rude. You bring your parrot over and leave it for several weeks, and maybe it will take up my parrot's good behavior."

So she did. Returning for it after a time she opened the door and walked in. Her parrot saw her and said, "I wish she was dead." Then the minister's parrot chimed in and said, "Amen, Lord, grant her request."

159. *Home* Sweet Home

A visiting minister remarked at the beginning of his sermon, that he felt right at home with them. "I saw all these empty seats up front, I felt the gum under my chair, and when I saw the size of the offerings, I knew I was among friends. You surely are my people."

160. *Resemblance*

A minister was making a pastoral call during which a mother asked, "Did you wear your robes when you visited the nursery class in church last Sunday?"

"Why, yes, why do you ask?" replied the pastor.

"Because of my son's report," the mother explained. "He came home and told the family, 'Something visited us today. It wasn't a witch, and it wasn't a clown. I don't know what it was.' "

161. *Free-Will* Offering

A mountaineer preacher down south was having considerable trouble meeting the church obligations. In desperation, he asked everyone who would give five dollars, to stand. "Now," he said, "will the organist play 'The Star Spangled Banner'?"

162. *Conditional* Agreement

Two ministers of different faiths were the best of friends, but often disagreed on religious issues. One day they had been arguing a little more than usual, on some theological point, when one of them said: "That's all right. We'll just agree to disagree. The thing that counts is that we're both doing the Lord's work . . . you in your way, and I in His."

163. *Cooperation*

An alert son of a minister was not inclined to allow sleeping in the church. One Sunday evening he perched himself in the gallery directly back of the pulpit.

Observing the eyes of the congregation centering there with lively interest, the pastor looked back just in time to see his offspring getting the range on a bald head in the fifth row of pews, with a paper wad.

"Keep on preaching, Dad," he called down, "and I will do my best to keep them awake."

F'r Instance

164. *A Bird* in the Hand

An old Southerner had worked on a plantation for his employer for many years, but left to become a preacher.

Some years later he returned for a visit. "I'm a preacher now," he told his boss.

"That's fine. Do you take notes for your preaching?" inquired his employer.

"No, sir," he replied. "I used to take notes at first, but now I demand the cash."

165. *Interest*

A minister was invited out to dinner one day, and he noticed a big dog in the corner keeping a sharp eye on him. Every time he took a bite the dog's eye followed his hand. He exclaimed, "This surely is the most intelligent dog I ever saw. He seems to be interested in my every bite."

"Yes, he is. You see, you are eating out of his plate."

166. *Active* Membership

"How many members do you have in your church?" a friend of the pastor inquired.

"Three hundred," replied the pastor.

"Are all of them active?" asked the friend.

"Yes," replied the pastor. "One hundred and seventy-five are working for me, and the other hundred and twenty-five are working against me."

167. Faith Without *Works*

A worldly-wise minister was having trouble collecting money from his congregation for a new addition to the church. Yet members kept telling him they were praying for the project's success. Donations finally went up one Sunday when a slogan appeared on the collection plate: "Pay now, Pray later!"

168. *Pessimism*

A golfing clergyman had taken a trimming from a parishioner thirty years his senior and was not happy about it.

"Cheer up," said his opponent. "Remember, you'll win at the finish. You'll probably be burying me one of these days."

"Even then," the minister answered gloomily, "it will still be your hole!"

169. *Substitute* Speaker

It was announced in church one day that a substitute preacher would preach.

A little boy leaned over and asked his mother, "What is a substitute?"

"Well, for example son, if you threw your baseball through the window and broke it, and we didn't have another real pane, we could put a piece of cardboard in the window . . . that's what we call a substitute."

When the substitute minister had finished preaching that morning, the little boy leaned over and said, "Mother, this sure isn't a substitute . . . he's a real *pain!*"

170. Come to *Point*

The janitor had dropped a box of tacks in the pulpit of the church.

"Now, what if you should miss picking up all those tacks and I should step on one during my sermon?" the aggravated minister asked.

"Sir," replied the janitor, "I bet that's one point you wouldn't linger on."

171. *Long-winded*

The new minister's first sermon lasted only fifteen minutes. His second one lasted thirty minutes—but his third sermon lasted about two hours.

A meeting was called by the Board to inquire of him why the length of the sermons was so varied.

"I will explain," said the minister. "The first time I had just had all my teeth pulled, and my mouth was sore."

"The second sermon was just after I had my new dentures fitted and I was having difficulty keeping them in."

"But the third sermon I accidentally picked up my wife's teeth by mistake."

172. By *Fruits*

Mary's parents, who had been opposing her desire to marry a young seminary student because they were afraid of the inability of a minister to provide for her as she had been accustomed. However they finally agreed to the marriage after hearing him preach.

"Was it my preaching that convinced you?" asked the young man.

"Yes," they answered. "When we heard you preach one sermon we knew you'd never make a preacher."

173. Long *Sermon*

The preacher had been delivering a dry, long-winded discourse, completely oblivious it seemed, to the restlessness of his congregation.

He was brought back quickly to earth, as a small boy sitting in the front pew lamented in a shrill voice: "Mommy, are you sure this is the only way we can get to heaven?"

174. Her *Pastor*

The minister's little daughter was sent to bed with a stomach-ache, and missed her usual romp with her daddy. A few minutes later she appeared at the top of the stairs and called to her mother: "Mama, let me talk with daddy."

"No, my dear, not tonight. Get back in bed."

"Please, mama."

"I said no. That's enough now."

"Mother, I'm a very sick woman, and I must see my pastor at once."

175. *Classified*

A minister in a small rural church surprised his congregation one Sunday morning by beginning his sermon thus:

"Friends, I have prepared a $50 sermon, a $20 sermon and a $10 sermon. We will now take up the offering and see which one it will be."

176. *Liberality*

A hat was passed around a certain congregation for the purpose of taking up an offering for the visiting minister.

Presently it was returned to him—emphatically and embarrassingly empty. Slowly and deliberately the parson inverted the hat and shook it meaningly. Then, raising his eyes to heaven, he exclaimed fervently: "I thank Thee, dear Lord, that I got my hat back from this congregation."

177. *Sudden* Change

A party of clergymen was attending a Presbyterian conference in Scotland. Several of them set off to explore the district. Presently they came to a river spanned by a temporary bridge. Not seeing the notice that said it was unsafe, they began to cross it. The bridge keeper ran after them in protest.

"It is all right," declared the spokesman, not understanding the reason for the old man's haste, "we're Presbyterians from the conference."

"I'm no' caring aboot that," was the reply, "but if ye dinna get off the bridge you'll all be Baptists!"

178. *Long-winded*

A minister pleasantly surprised his congregation by delivering a ten-minute sermon instead of the usual thirty-minute message.

In concluding, he explained, "I regret to inform you, brethren, that my dog, who appears to be inordinately fond of paper, this morning ate that portion of sermon which I have not delivered. Let us pray."

After the services a visitor from another church, approached the pastor and said, "Preacher, please let me know if that dog of yours has any pups. If it does, I want to buy one for my minister."

179. *Similarity*

The preacher, hoping to get acquainted with one of the new members of the congregation, knocked on the front door of her home one evening.

"Is that you, Angel?" came the woman's voice from within.

"No," replied the minister, "but I'm from the same department."

180. *Stability*

The Rabbi and the Priest were eating together.

Priest: "Doctor Cohen, when are you going to be sensible enough to enjoy this delicious ham with me?"

Rabbi: At your wedding, Father Kelly. At your wedding."

181. Get the *Facts*

Three religious leaders, a Jewish Rabbi, a Catholic Priest, and a Protestant minister, respectively, went fishing together in a small boat. The Rabbi, suddenly remembering he had left his fishing pole at the cabin, stepped out of the boat and walked on the water to the shore.

Just then, the Priest remarked that he had left his lure behind, and he too, stepped over the side of the boat, and followed in the same direction as the Rabbi.

When they both returned to the boat, the Protestant minister who had watched this remarkable demonstration, reasoned, "Now, my faith must be as strong as theirs." Determinedly he stepped out into the water—and immediately sank to the bottom.

His two companions dragged him out, but once again he made a determined effort of faith, and again sank into the water.

"My faith must be as strong as yours; why can't I walk on the water like you?" he sputteringly asked his rescuers.

The Rabbi turned to the Priest and said, "We'd better tell him where those rocks are before he drowns himself."

182. Bad *Loser*

Once, during the Civil War, a traveling evangelist asked for the privilege of conducting a campfire service for a New York outfit, adding that the night before he had made eight converts in a neighboring regiment.

"Is that so?" said the New York Colonel. Then turning to one of his officers he ordered:

"Captain, detail ten of your men for baptism. No Massachusetts regiment is going to beat mine for piety."

183. No *Relation*

Parson Jones phoned the local board of health to have a dead mule removed from his lawn. The young clerk, who took the phone call, thought he'd be smart, and said: "I thought you ministers took care of the dead."

"We do," answered the parson, "but first we get in touch with the relatives."

184. Pre-*judging*

A new pastor in town was introduced at the Rotary Club, and he was invited to join.

Unfortunately, his category was filled and the only category open was for a hog-caller, and it was suggested he join under this classification.

"Well," he said, "I've always been classed as a Shepherd of the Sheep, but I suppose you know your own people better than I do."

185. Top *Secret*

A young ministerial student was traveling on a train, and beside him sat an old, rural minister.

The young man said: "I'm preparing notes on my sermon for next Sunday."

The old preacher said: "Son, you shouldn't do that. Never make notes because the devil might look over your shoulder and read them, so he'll be prepared too. Take me now, son," he added, "I think a little while I'm plowing on what I'm going to say, but when Sunday comes even the Lord Himself don't know what I'm going to say."

186. Taking No *Chances*

A minister was phoned by a sick lady who was active in a church of another denomination. She asked him if he would be kind enough to come to her bedside.

When he arrived the minister said to the lady's ten-year-old son: "I'm most happy your mother called me. Only tell me is your minister out of town?"

"Not at all," replied the little shaver. "Mommy just said she was afraid she might have a sickness that was contagious."

Parade

187. Getting *Personal*

A minister was on a train when a well-dressed woman boarded. "Ah, here is an opportunity for discussing spiritual matters," he thought to himself.

However, for almost an hour she talked incessantly, about her family, her clothes, her illnesses and her operation.

Finally, as she paused for a moment, the minister asked, "May I inquire about your religious life, madam?"

"Sir," she replied indignantly, "I am not in the habit of discussing my personal life with strangers!"

"Madam," replied the minister, "after listening to you for the past hour, I know you both inside and out."

188. *Preaching*

The story is told of a preacher who went to the mountains to preach, and upon arriving struck up a conversation with the first old man he met.

"Are you a Christian?" the preacher inquired.

"Nope, Mr. Christian lives up the 'holler,' " answered the mountaineer.

"What I mean is, Brother, are you lost?" persisted the preacher.

"Well, I reckon not," replied the mountaineer. "I have been here nigh on to thirty years and know every cow path in these here hills."

"You don't understand," said the preacher. "I mean are you ready for the Judgment Day?"

"When's it comin'?" asked the mountaineer.

"Well," said the preacher, "it might come today or it might be tomorrow."

"For goodness sakes, don't tell my missus," cautioned the mountaineer. "She'd want to go both days!"

189. *Liars*

A minister in a small church said, "Today, I'm preaching on the 29th chapter of Matthew. How many in the congregation have read it?"

Nearly every hand in the church went up.

"Yes, you are the folks who need my sermon. There is no 29th chapter of Matthew. My subject is 'Liars.' "

190. *Mis-quotations*

A preacher was quoting a verse about visiting the sick, raising the dead, and casting out devils. He got a little mixed up and said: "The Bible admonishes us to *cast out the sick . . . heal the dead . . . and raise the devil.*"

191. Meeting too *Long*

The new minister found only one person at his first rural Sunday night service. "What do you think we should do about the service," he asked the man, "inasmuch as we have such a small congregation."

The man replied. "Well, sir, I have never been to school very much. I don't have much education and I don't know much about the Bible, but this one thing I know, that when I promise my cows a load of hay, I always keep my promise."

"Well, come in then, and we will have a service," said the minister. The minister was long-winded, and it was an exceptionally long service. Afterward the minister asked the farmer, "What did you think of the service?"

"Well," he said, "I have never been to school, I'm not educated, and I don't know much about the Bible, but this one thing I know, when I promise my cows a load of hay and only one shows up, I never give it the whole load."

192. Real *Sacrifice*

An elderly lady attended a church after a rather long absence. She noticed a bronze plaque in the vestibule of the church, and after the service asked the minister what it was.

He explained that it was a memorial to the men who served in the services.

"What are the years beside some of the names?" she asked.

"Those are the ones who died in the Service," replied the minister.

"Which one, pastor, the 9:30 or 11:00 o'clock service?

COOPERATION

193. *Cooperation*

A man met a pretty girl and fell in love with her. He took her rowing one day and she fell overboard.

He grabbed her hair, and a wig came off in his hands. He reached for her arm and an artificial arm came off likewise.

He said, "Listen, sweetheart, if I'm going to be able to help you, you must cooperate a little."

194. *Consideration*

The car crunched to a stop on the busy parkway as the driver noticed a lady standing beside a car, looking help-lessly at a flat tire.

The driver came over and started removing the tire.

Woman (*murmuring gratefully*): "Oh, thank you. I don't know a blessed thing about these things."

Man: "You don't have to, ma'am ... it's no job for a lady."

After the tire was changed, the woman put her finger up to her lips, saying: "Let the jack down easy, won't you? My husband's taking a nap in the back seat."

195. *Sympathy*

"Madam," he addressed her in a broken voice, "I wish to draw your attention to the terrible plight of a poor family in this district. The father is dead, the mother is too ill to work, and the nine children are starving. They are about to be turned out into the cold, cold streets unless someone pays their arrears in rent which amounts to fifty dollars."

"How terrible," exclaimed the lady. "May I ask you who you are?" The sympathetic visitor applied his handkerchief to his eyes as he said, "I'm the landlord."

A Bit of Honey

196. Your *Help* Needed

A man riding an airplane suddenly discovered two motors on one side were on fire. He began to cry at the top of his voice, "Two motors on fire, two motors on fire."

Panic spread fast among the passengers.

Then suddenly the pilot appeared at the door, with a large parachute strapped securely on his back.

"Now don't you worry," he said. "I'm going for help."

197. Some Always *Kick*

A man was going home late at night and taking a short cut through the graveyard. He stepped into a newly dug grave.

"Help! I'm cold . . . help, I'm cold," he cried plaintively.

A somewhat inebriated passer-by heard his cries and grabbing a shovel, started throwing dirt into the grave.

"Of course you're cold!" he said, "You kicked all the dirt off you."

198. Doing His *Part*

The bus was jammed when an extremely overweight lady entered. She stood and stared at all the seated passengers.

"Isn't there a gentleman in this bus," she demanded loudly, "who will offer me a seat?"

A small sailor jumped up. "Well," he volunteered, "I'm willing to make a contribution."

Parade

199. Following *Orders*

A young man wanted to pass an old man in a wagon on a country road, but the old man wouldn't pull over.

Finally, when he had passed the old man, he took his pistol out and walked back to the wagon. "Old man, do you know how to dance?" he asked, shooting at the ground near his feet and laughing uproariously, as the old man began to jump up and down.

The young man started back when the old man grabbed

his concealed shotgun and said, "Young man, did you ever kiss a mule?"

The young man said, looking into the barrel of the shot gun, "No, but I always wanted to."

200. *Giving With a Purpose*

A big company executive attended a United Fund meeting and pledged one hundred per cent co-operation from all his employees.

After the meeting, he returned to his company and instructed his manager to collect a contribution from all his employees as he had promised.

After three days the manager reported that all had given with the exception of John Jones who refused to give in spite of all his persuading.

"Have him come to my office," the big executive instructed.

"Jones, I hear that you have refused to contribute to the United Fund," the executive said.

"Yes sir," replied John Jones. "I never do give to it."

"Jones, I have promised that all will contribute and you will either do so or be fired," thundered the chief.

John Jones meekly took out his billfold and laid a fifty-dollar bill on the executive's desk.

"I would have given sooner but nobody ever explained it the way you did before," he added.

201. *Helpful*

A man walking down a street on a dark night passed an alley. Two thugs jumped on him, and though he put up a terrific fight, they got him down.

After they searched him, they were amazed at the small amount of money they found in his pockets. "You mean you put up that fight for sixty-seven cents?" they asked.

"Shucks, no," answered the victim. "I thought you were after the $500 in my shoe."

202. *Warning*

An old farmer with an ill temper, married. Soon after the wedding they visited a nearby town. Suddenly the mule pulling the wagon stopped, and the farmer angrily pointed to the mule and said: "Now, that's one!"

Later the mule stopped again and rared up. "Now, that's two!" exclaimed the farmer in a loud voice. Soon the old mule stopped again and the farmer angrily cried, "Now, that's three!" and shot the mule between the eyes.

The new bride said, "Now, honey, that wasn't necessary. The mule was doing the best it could, I don't think you are fair."

The old farmer quickly pointed to his new bride and said: "Now, that's one!"

203. *Complimentary*

An elderly mountaineer woman was having difficulty in getting her horse to pull its heavily loaded cart up the hill. Observing her plight, the village lawyer got behind it and pushed both horse and cart over the top.

"Thank you," she said appreciatively. "I'd never have done it with just one donkey."

DEFINITIONS

204. *Stubborn*

A small boy wrote an essay on the mule as follows: "The mule is a hardier bird than the goose or turkey. It has two legs to walk with, two more to kick with, and wears its wings on the side of its head. It is stubbornly backward about going forward."

205. Modern *Music*

A sad commentary on our modern music occurred when someone in a "Juke Joint" dropped a tray of plates and seven couples got up to dance.

206. *Modernism*

A modern preacher said: "If you don't *repent* (in a manner), you'll be *damned* (generally speaking) . . . and go to *hell* (in a degree)."

207. *Human Nature*

Someone said: "People are funny. They want the front of the bus, the back of the church and the middle of the road."

208. *Optimism*

An optimist fell out of a ten story building. As he passed the second floor he was heard to say, "Safe so far."

A Bit of Honey

209. *Irritation* Plus

Irritation . . . is when a man calls you on the telephone about 1:00 A.M. and says, "I want to speak to Joe." "He doesn't live here," you tell him sleepily.

Aggravation . . . is when the same voice calls back at 2:00 A.M. and says, "Are you sure Joe doesn't live there?"

Frustration . . . is when a voice calls at 3:00 A.M. and says, "I'm Joe. Do I have any calls?"

210. Building Air *Castles*

A psychiatrist was explaining the difference between a psychotic and a neurotic.

"A psychotic is one who builds air castles and a neurotic lives in them."

A voice from the back of the audience said, "Yes, and a psychiatrist collects the rent on both of them."

DOCTORS—PATIENTS

211. Early *Symptoms*

A hypochondriac told his doctor in great alarm that he was sure he had a fatal liver disease.

"Nonsense!" protested the doctor. "You would never know if you had the disease or not. With that ailment there's no discomfort of any kind."

"I know," gasped the patient. "My symptoms exactly."

Parade

212. Majoring on the *Minors*

A woman was seriously ill. Her husband summoned the doctor, who dashed inside the sickroom and came out a minute later asking for a chisel. The stunned but anxious husband didn't ask questions. He found a chisel.

Minutes later the doctor poked his head out and asked, "You got a hammer?"

The husband was puzzled, but not wanting to doubt the doctor, gave him a hammer. Five minutes later out came the doctor asking for hacksaw.

By now the husband was completely upset and screamed hysterically, "Doctor, you asked for a hammer, a chisel and a hacksaw. What are you doing to my wife?"

"What wife?" asked the doctor. "I'm trying to open my satchel!"

Parade

213. *Strains* of Life

After the doctor checked the patient over, he asked, "Have you been living a normal life?"

"Yes, doctor," replied the patient.

"Well, you'll have to cut it out for a while."

214. By *Association*

A high official, trying unsuccessfully to get a long distance call through from an insane asylum, became exasperated.

Finally, addressing the operator, in a not-too-pleasant voice, he asked: "Young lady, do you know who I am?"

"No, sir," was the sweet reply, "but I know *where* you are."

215. *Regular* Patient

The doctor's visits were twelve dollars for the first call, and three for each additional call.

Sandy was taken ill for the first time in his life and had to call a doctor to his bedside.

Raising his head weakly from his pillow he greeted the doctor with: "Doctor, I sure am happy to have you visit me once again."

216. Good *Foundation*

Patient (talking to a nurse in doctor's office): "I've got a bad case of arthritis; there's a painful buzzing in my ears; I have a sprained ankle; my thumb is out of joint; and I see spots before my eyes. . . ."

Admiringly, the nurse replied: "But you must be awfully healthy to stand all that pain."

217. Always *Right*

An elderly man visited a doctor for a thorough physical examination. Upon finishing the examination, the doctor said, "You're as fit as a fiddle. You'll live to be eighty."

"But, I am eighty!" said the patient.

The doctor smiled, "See, what did I tell you?"

Parade

218. *Sympathy*

A hypochondriac became discouraged because no one seemed to take his ailments seriously, so he ordered this inscription for his gravestone: "Now will you believe I'm sick?"

Parade

218. *Illusion*

"Please help me, Doctor," the patient said to the psychiatrist. "I have this terrible feeling that I am a dog. All the time I'm a dog."

The psychiatrist thought for a moment. "Tell me, young man," he asked. "How long have you felt like that?"

"Ever since I was a puppy."

Parade

220. Easy to *Replace*

An employee broke his leg and was visited by a fellow worker in the hospital. The fellow worker, consoling the friend, said, "The boss said just take it easy and he would get someone to do your job, just as soon as he finds out what you did."

221. *Nervousness*

The doctor, after examining the patient, said, "Your nerves are bad. I wouldn't be surprised if you drink seven or eight cups of coffee a day."

The patient tremblingly said, "Doc, I spill that many."

222. *Chatter Box*

Sam's wife had injured her jaw and had to visit the emergency department at the local hospital.

"Did they take an x-ray photo of your wife's jaw at the hospital?" an interested friend inquired.

"They tried to," explained Sam, "but they ended up with a moving picture."

223. Poor *Recovery*

A business man explained to his physician: "I can't pay my bill, Doc! I slowed down just like you told me to, and I lost my job."

224. I Feel Like A *Sick* Mule

A farmer had a very sick mule, so he called the veterinarian. He took his little black bag, and upon arrival, took the mule's pulse, temperature, and all the things that you do when you examine a sick mule.

The vet said, "This is a very sick mule, and I want you to give it these little white pills immediately. These white ones are very potent, and will cure practically anything a sick mule has.

"But, just to be sure, wait four hours and give the mule one of these red pills. They are so strong, they will cure anything."

The farmer and doctor met in about two weeks, and the doctor asked the farmer what happened to the mule.

"Well, I gave him the white pills like you told me, Doc. And I never saw so much reaction from one mule in all my life. He kicked down the barn door—the back fence and took off across the country. I thought I had lost my mule."

"Did you lose him," the doctor asked.

"You know, Doc, if I hadn't had the presence of mind to take that red pill myself, that mule would have been long gone."

225. Money's *Worth*

Sandy was having trouble with a toothache, so he decided to visit the dentist.

"What do you charge for extracting a tooth?" Sandy asked.

"Five dollars," replied the dentist.

"Five dollars for only two seconds' work?" exclaimed Sandy.

"Well," replied the dentist, "if you wish, I can extract it very slowly."

226. Patient *Patience*

A man in the dentist's chair cried; "Here Doc, you haven't pulled the right tooth!"

The doctor replied calmly, "I know it, my man, but I'm coming to it."

F'r Instance

227. *Advice*

A doctor asked his new patient if she had been to any other doctor about her complaint, before coming to see him.

"No," she replied, and then added, "But I did go to see my druggist."

"Well, that shows just how much sense some people have!" he exclaimed.

"And what sort of idiotic advice did your druggist give you?"

"Oh," she answered sweetly, "he told me to see you."

Parade

228. *Guessing* Game

A surgeon examined a new patient most carefully. After studying the x-rays, he turned to the man and said, "Could you pay for an operation if I told you it was necessary?"

The patient thought for a moment, then said to the doctor: "Would you find one necessary if I told you I couldn't pay for it?"

Parade

229. Unbalanced *Budget*

A fellow went to a very high-priced psychiatrist and said, "Doc, I've got a problem."

"What's your problem?" asked the doctor.

"Well, I'm married, I've got a car, my wife has a car, we have three children, we have a home in the country and a home in the city."

"You don't seem so bad off," replied the doctor. "What's your problem?"

The patient cried out, "I only make $45 a week."

Parade

230. Get at the *Source*

The doctor told the patient's wife, "Your husband must have rest and quiet. I am going to prescribe these sleeping pills."

"Thank you, Doctor," said the wife, "when do I give them to him?"

"Oh," said the doctor, "I don't mean to give them to him. I want you to take them yourself."

231. Profit *Sharing*

A rich old man had been visiting his psychiatrist every day, for several months. He lay on the couch and went to sleep every time. After he awoke he paid the $25.00 fee for each visit.

The doctor was disturbed at his never talking and one day said, "Now I want you to think of something and ask me about it."

After a few minutes of silence, suddenly, the old man bolted up right from the couch. The doctor said, "Do you have something to ask?"

"Yes," replied the old man, "you don't need a partner do you?"

232. *Fortune Telling*

The doctors are pretty expensive these days. A few weeks ago I fell down a flight of stairs and hurt my leg. So, I went to a doctor. He fixed me up and said, "Don't worry! you'll be walking before the day is over."

He was right . . . I had to sell my car in order to pay him.

Parade

233. Patient's *Patience*

There had been an epidemic of influenza in the town. A physician who had almost no sleep for a week called upon a patient who was suffering from pneumonia.

"Begin counting," directed the doctor as he leaned over to hear the patient's respiration.

The doctor was so fatigued he fell asleep with his head on the sick man's chest.

It seemed but a moment when he awoke suddenly to hear the patient still counting, "10,888—10,889. . . ."

234. Follow *Orders*

A local doctor became quite popular over night when he was "written up" in a large city paper.

He was approached soon afterward by a middle-aged woman, who gushed: "Oh, Doctor, I guess you don't remember me. Twenty years ago you came to see me at home and told me to stay in bed until you called back again. But you never came back!"

The doctor answered briskly: "Well then, what are you doing out of bed?"

235. My *First* Aid

"I'm so grateful for my first-aid training," exclaimed the girl. "Last night there was an accident right in front of my house. An old man was knocked down by a car and was bleeding all over. He was moaning something awful. That's when my first-aid training came in handy. I remembered to put my head between my knees to keep from fainting."

236. S. O. S.

The fellow in the oxygen tent was definitely on the danger list. His pastor entered the room; the patient began to gasp for air, frantically.

"Don't worry now, friend," the pastor said, "the church is praying for you, your wife will be looked after, and we will try to take care of your business. Now is there anything else I can do for you?"

Gasping for breath, the patient said, "Yes, will you *please move, you are standing on the air hose!*"

237. *Improvement*

I was speaking in a mental institution a few years ago. During my talk a fellow said: *"Rotten."* Later, he said, a little louder: *"Rotten."* Then quite loud: *"Rottener."*

I said to the superintendent, "Can't this man be quieted down? This is very annoying."

"No," he said, "this makes me very happy. This is the first intelligent word this man has spoken in ten years!"

238. *Misery Likes* Company

A woman had been bitten by a mad dog and looked as if

she were going to die. The Pasteur treatment wasn't working. The doctor told her she had better make her will. Taking her pen and paper she began to write. In fact, she wrote and wrote.

Finally, the doctor said, "This is surely a lengthy will you are making."

"Will nothing," she raved. "I'm making a list of all the people I'm going to bite."

239. *Revenge*

A fellow went to the hospital to visit his dying partner.

Suddenly the dying man began to speak. "John," he said, "before I go I must confess some things. I know I am going to die. I want you to know that I robbed the firm of $80,000 several years ago. I sold our secret formula to our competitors, and also, John, I'm the fellow who supplied your wife with the evidence that got her a divorce and cost you a small fortune."

John murmured, "That's okay, old man. I'm the guy who poisoned you."

240. *Two in One*

A doctor was called and asked to visit an old man who lived quite a way out of town.

The wife, doing the calling, said, "Doctor, I hate to ask you to come so far, but my husband is very sick."

"Oh, that's quite all right," he replied. "I have another patient in the neighborhood, so I'll just come out and kill two birds with one stone."

241. Concrete *Evidence*

A visitor to an insane asylum found one of the inmates rocking back and forth in a chair in a contented manner, cooing repeatedly, "Lulu, Lulu. . . ."

"What's the matter with this man?" the visitor asked the attendant.

"Well, you see, sir, Lulu was the woman who jilted him," the attendant explained.

Baffled with the explanation, the visitor proceeded on the tour.

Later he came to a padded cell, where an inmate was

batting his head repeatedly against the wall and crying, "Lulu, Lulu. . . ."

"Now why is that man crying 'Lulu'?" asked the visitor.

"Oh, he's the fellow Lulu finally married," the attendant explained.

242. *Appearances*

An old man was very sick. He thought he was going to die, so he called for a Bible. "Bring it quick, I'm dying," he gasped.

Someone brought the big family Bible, with a mirror on the cover, and handed it to him.

As he looked into the mirror he cried, "Never mind ... it's too late ... the devil got ahead of me."

243. Clean *Sweep*

At a meeting of senior citizens, the speaker reached the climax of his talk and declared with fervor: "The time has come when we must get rid of socialism and communism and anarchism, and—"

At that point, a little old lady at the rear of the room arose feebly but with enthusiasm, and, waving her cane in the air, shouted; "And let's throw out rheumatism, too!"

Parade

244. *Hope*

"I sure hope I'm sick," said the unhappy man to his doctor. "I'd sure hate to feel like this if I'm well!"

245. Divine *Gift*

"I'm afraid, doctor," said a woman to her physician, "that my husband has some terrible mental affliction." She paused a moment and then continued, "Sometimes I talk to him for hours and then discover that he literally hasn't heard a word I said."

"That isn't an affliction," replied the doctor, "that's a divine gift."

A Bit of Honey

246. Just *Checking*

Recently my brother was told that he'd have to undergo a kidney operation.

"Let me advise you now," said the surgeon, "of how I work. I believe in getting my patients up and around very quickly. Three hours following the operation you'll sit up. Five hours after, you'll stand up. The next day you'll be walking."

"Fine," my brother agreed. "But will you let me lie down during the operation?"

Parade

247. Expedient

The lady visited the doctor's office every week with a new complaint, although, in fact, she was in fine health. This week her ailment was that she was growing hard of hearing.

"It's so bad," she said, "I can't hear myself cough."

The doctor nodded patiently and filled out a prescription.

"Will this improve my hearing?" the lady asked.

"No," replied the doctor, "but it will help you to cough louder."

EMPLOYMENT—WORK

248. Making *Decisions*

An old farmer hired a local boy to sort the Irish potatoes. He asked him to separate the potatoes in three piles, one for the small ones, one for the medium ones, and one for the large ones. After a couple of hours the hired man said he was quitting the job. His brow was wet with perspiration and he seemed very flustered.

The farmer asked him why he was quitting. "Is the work too hard for you?"

"No," he answered, "but the decisions are killing me."

249. *Imagination*

Employer: "Look here, what did you mean by telling me you had five year's experience when you've never even had a job before?"

Young man: "Well, you advertised for a man with imagination."

250. *Safety* First

An old Georgia cracker sat barefooted on the steps of his tumbledown shack, smoking a corncob pipe.

A stranger stopped for a drink of water. Wishing to be agreeable he asked, "How is your cotton coming on?"

"Ain't got none," said the cracker.

"Didn't you plant any?" asked the stranger.

"Nope," was the reply; " 'fraid o' boll weevils."

"Well," asked the stranger, "how is your corn?"

"Didn't plant none," replied the native; " 'fraid there wa'nt goin' to be no rain."

The visitor was abashed, but cheerful still. "Well, how are your potatoes?"

"Ain't got none; scairt o' potato bugs—pow'rful lot ub'm here."

"Well, really, what did you plant?" asked the stranger.

"Nothin', jes playin' safe."

A Bit of Honey

251. *Conditional*

An executive revealed the absolute fairness of his boss. At a meeting the other day, he put several ideas before his staff.

"All of you who find yourselves in disagreement with the suggestions I have made," he announced at the finish, "will please signify by saying, 'I resign.' "

252. *Efficiency*

An efficiency expert died and on the way to the grave, raised the lid of the coffin and said: "If you will put wheels on this box you can lay off four men."

Parade

253. Checking on *Job*

A young boy rushed into a service station to use the telephone. "Sir, do you have need of a young boy to work for you?" he was heard to inquire. "You don't! You've already got a good boy? Thank you, sir."

With that he hung up the receiver and started to leave, whistling merrily.

The attendant was surprised. "Why are you whistling

after you heard they already have a good boy and do not need you? What makes you so happy?"

"Well," said the boy, "I'm the good boy that they've got, and I was just checking on my job."

254. In Line of *Duty*

A patrolman, walking his beat spotted a man climbing a bridge. The man stood on the edge of the rail looking out at the river beneath. The patrolman shed his coat, dashed to the bridge, climbed up and pleaded with the man to come down.

Finally the man did, and the patrolman said to him, "Why did you do that, buddy?"

The man answered calmly, "It's my job, officer. I'm inspector of public works."

Parade

255. *Laziness*

A young farmer had a father-in-law who would not work. The young man got tired of supporting the old man in idleness and he took steps. He decided that he might just as well bury the loafer. He made a wooden coffin, put the old man in, and started off with it in his wagon toward the graveyard.

A neighbor, who had heard of his plan, intercepted him. "You really oughtn't do that," he said. "Here are two bushels of corn. Take your father-in-law back home and let him eat that up at any rate."

The old man raised his head up out of the coffin. "Neighbor," he said, "is that corn shucked?"

"No," replied the neighbor.

"Drive on, son," replied the old man.

256. Taking no *Chances*

A wealthy man was interviewing a chauffeur. "I want a chauffeur that doesn't take the slightest risk," he explained.

"I'm your man, sir," said the prospective employee. "Can I have my salary in advance?"

257. *Jealousy*

A man working on a road group complained he had worked two weeks and hadn't been given a shovel.

"Well," said the foreman, "you are getting paid aren't you?"

"That's not the problem," interjected the man. "All the other men around here have something to lean on."

258. *Indolence*

A tramp stopped by a nice house to ask for a meal.

The lady said, "Do you see that pile of wood that needs sawing?"

"I see it," he said.

"Well?" She paused.

"Lady," grinned the tramp, *"you saw me see it,* but you ain't gonna *see me saw it."*

259. *Training*-on-the-Job

A fellow walked into a watch company and asked for a job that paid $100 a week. But after talking to the manager about it, he announced that he wanted $200 a week.

The manager was puzzled, and said, "Have you ever done precision work before?"

"No," he replied.

"Well, why do you want $200 instead of one hundred?"

The fellow explained, "Because it's harder when you don't know how to do it."

260. *Qualifications*

A fellow went to Washington for an interview regarding a political appointment.

"What can you do?" asked the big shot.

"Nothing," replied the fellow.

"That's wonderful," was the reply. "Then we won't have to break you in."

261. Positive *Proof*

A leading citizen was stopped by a panhandler. "Listen, buddy," the leading citizen said, "why don't you try working for a living? After all, work never killed anybody."

"You're wrong, friend," the panhandler said. "I've lost two wives that way."

Parade

262. No *Ambition*

I walked by a panhandler the other day, and he said, "Hey, Mac, give me a buck, will ya?"

I asked, "Aren't you ashamed to stand in the street begging for money?"

"Listen," he answered, "whattya want me to do ... open up an office?"

263. *Mistaken Identity*

The owner of a store was passing through the packing room and saw a boy lounging against a box whistling cheerfully. Thinking of all his money being wasted on this kind of labor, the employer asked gruffly: "How much do you get a week?"

"Ten dollars," replied the boy.

"Here's your pay for the week," said the man. "Now get out."

On his way back to the office, the owner ran into the foreman and asked him: "When did we hire that boy, and who is responsible?"

"We never hired him," said the foreman. "He was just delivering a package from another firm."

264. *Lazy* Man

Up in the mountains a man won the title of "the laziest man." A gentleman from the sponsoring company came to deliver the $1,000 prize.

When the door opened he said, "Where is Mr. Jackson, the laziest man in the world?"

"He's down by the creek," was the reply.

He found him lying down, not moving a muscle, with eyes closed.

"I have your $1,000 as prize and I want to give it to you."

"Roll me over and put it in my left pocket," said the mountaineer.

265. *Kind* Words

Customer to waitress: "I'm both hungry and tired. All I want for breakfast is two soft-boiled eggs, coffee and some kind words."

A bit later: "I have the eggs and the coffee—but where are the kind words?"

Waitress: "Don't eat them eggs."

266. *Diversity*

"Can you serve company?" asked the wealthy matron when she was hiring a new maid.

"Yes, ma'am, both ways."

"What do you mean?" asked the puzzled woman.

"So they'll come again or stay away."

EXPLANATIONS

267. Final *Authority*

Three baseball umpires were discussing the game.

First Umpire: "I calls 'em as I sees 'em."

Second Umpire: "They is what I calls 'em."

Third Umpire: "They ain't nothin 'til I calls 'em."

268. Limited *Knowledge*

A fellow from the hills of East Tennessee, who was appearing in a lawsuit, was being questioned as to his educational qualifications by the plaintiff's lawyer.

"Can you write?" asked the lawyer.

"Nope."

"Can you read?"

"Wa'al, I can read figgers pretty well, but I don't do so good with my writin'."

"How is that?"

"Wa'al, take these signs along the road when I want to go somewhere; I kin read how fur, but not whare."

269. *Sucker*

Two modern misses were talking together: "I'm looking for a dashing cavalier," one of them said.

"A cavalier," inquired the other, "what's that?"

The young lady explained: "A cavalier is a fellow who comes for you in a big Cadillac, brings flowers and candy each time he visits, takes you to dine in the best restaurant in town, drives you home, then bows at the door and kisses your hand."

"That's a cavalier?" asked the other incredulously. "Why, we've got hundreds of them in our neighborhood, but we call them 'suckers.'"

270. *Pronunciation*

A woman treasurer, after attending the Women's Aid meeting, took the money to the bank, all tied up in her handkerchief.

She said, "Here is our Aid money."

The banker thought she said "egg money" . . . and he said, "You sure have some nice old hens."

271. *Vindication*

A Southerner was asked, "How did we lose the war if we won so many battles?"

An old-timer said, "We just wore ourselves out whipping the enemy."

272. Big *Mouth*

The little man from Mars landed in front of a music store. He looked at one of the pianos in the window and growled, "All right, wise guy. Wipe that smile off your face and take me to your leader."

273. Modern *Miracle*

This tale of guile and deception was related by a Customs Inspector in San Francisco.

A little old lady was stopped as she was passing through the Customs House and the Inspector asked her what she had in a bottle in her valise.

"Holy water," she replied in a thick Irish brogue.

The Inspector uncorked the bottle and sniffed at it. "But this is Irish whisky," he exclaimed.

"Saints be praised!" said the little old lady, " 'tis a miracle."

Parade

274. *Sooner* the Better

A man delivered a talk and a dear lady said, "Oh, how good your speech was! Will it appear in print!"

He thought a moment and said, "No, I suppose not. But if it is, it will be posthumously."

"Well," said she, "I hope it will be soon."

275. *Late for Meeting*

A man in a low-slung sports car was cruising along at about 90 miles an hour on Highway 89.

A motorcycle patrolman finally caught up with him, stopped him, and growled: "Say, buddy, didn't you see the speed limit posted back there?"

"Why, yes, officer," replied the speeder. "I saw the sign and I thought it said 89 miles per hour."

"Brother," the cop sighed, "I'm sure glad I caught up with you before you turned onto Highway 301."

276. In *Comparison*

Judge: "So, you are charged again with being drunk and disorderly. They have your first name listed as 'Major.' Have you ever been in the Service?"

Prisoner: "Yes, sir."

Judge: "Were you an officer?"

Prisoner: "No, sir."

Judge: "What does the 'Major' mean then?"

Prisoner: "To tell you the truth, sir, it doesn't mean a bit more than the 'Honorable' in front of your name."

277. On *Time*

A man went to the bus station to catch a bus, but found he was early. He saw a little fortune-telling machine—so he put a nickel in, and a little card came out that said, "You are John Jones—you are sixty-five years old—and you are on your way to Chicago on a business trip."

He said, "I don't believe this machine knows this information. There must be someone behind it." But he put another nickel in and another card came out saying, "You are John Jones—you are sixty-five years old—and you are on your way to Chicago on a business trip."

"I just don't believe it," said the man again, as he put another nickel in. This time a card came out saying: "You are still John Jones—you are still sixty-five years old—you are still on your way to Chicago—but you've fooled around and missed your bus."

278. No *Stirring*

A fellow ordered a cup of coffee in a restaurant, put ten heaping teaspoons of sugar in it and started to drink.

The waitress was puzzled: "Why don't you stir it up?" she asked.

He looked at her in a surprised sort of way and explained, "Miss, I just don't like my coffee sweet."

279. *Fed* Up

A case was being heard in court in which a farmer was claiming indemnity for a cow killed by a railroad train. Counsel for the defense put many tedious and superfluous questions.

"Was the cow on the track?" he asked the engineer again and again.

The engineer had had about enough. He replied, "No, of course not. She was in a field half a mile away. But when it saw her, the engine left the rails, jumped the fence and chased her across the field and up a tree. There it strangled her to death."

280. Some *Difference*

"Oh, what a strange looking cow," exclaimed the sweet young lady from Chicago, "but why hasn't she any horns?"

"Well, you see," explained the farmer, "some cows are born without horns and never had any, and others shed theirs, and some we dehorn, and some breeds aren't supposed to have horns at all. There's a lot of reasons why some cows ain't got horns, but the reason why that cow ain't got horns is because it ain't a cow . . . she's a horse."

281. Close *Association*

The prison warden felt sorry for one of his prisoners who never had visitors and remained alone in his cell on visiting days.

"Ben," he said kindly, "I notice you never have visitors. Don't you have any friends or family?"

"Oh, sure," replied Ben, "but they're all in here."

282. Meaningful *Nicknames*

At a large college, Professor Davis was talking to a small

group of students after class one day, and the name of a colleague was mentioned.

"I understand," he said, "that the boys have a nickname for Professor Brown. I think that is a great sign of affection and friendship. Someone told me they call him 'Maxwell House.' Is that correct?"

"Yes, it is," one of the boys replied.

"I wish they had one for me," said Professor Davis. "I'd take it as a great compliment."

"Oh, they have one for you already," said another boy. "They call you 'Sanka'."

Shortly afterward, Professor Davis happened to see advertising displays of the coffees named and examined them carefully. On the last Maxwell House display he found the words, "Good to the last drop," and on the "Sanka" label: "More than ninety-eight per cent of the active portion of the bean has been removed."

283. *Cause* and Effect

There were two friends—one thin and the other fat. They met one day, and the fat one said, "You look like you have been in a famine."

"Yes," replied the thin man, "and you look like you caused it!"

284. Cause and *Effect*

A surgeon, an architect and a politician were arguing about whose profession was the oldest.

Said the surgeon: "Eve was made from Adam's rib, and that surely was a surgical operation."

"Maybe," said the architect, "But prior to that, order was created out of chaos, and that was an architectural job."

"But," interrupted the politician, "somebody created the chaos first."

285. *Class Distinction*

"What is the difference between First, Second and Third Class travel?" asked the man at the ticket office of the local railroad.

"Well, sir," he was told, "when the stage coach gets stuck in the mud, the First Class passengers just sit, the

Second Class have to get out, and the Third Class help push."

286. Taking a *Dim View*

It had rained hard. The windshield was spattered with mud, the car had narrowly escaped several collisions, and the hitchhiker was beginning to regret that he had been picked up by this particular motorist.

"Wouldn't it be a good idea to wipe off the windshield?" he suggested anxiously.

"It wouldn't do a bit of good, son," said the cheerful driver, "I left my glasses at home."

287. Stretching *Imagination*

The retired colonel shot at a duck, while on a hunting trip, but missed by several yards.

"My, that's an absolute miracle!" said the colonel with a straight face. "There flies a dead duck!"

288. Wrong *Classification*

Two lions were in a zoo. One of them had been there for several years, while the second one was a newcomer.

At feeding time the new lion noticed that he received a few figs, nuts and bananas, while the older one was given a luscious, juicy chunk of meat.

After this had gone on for several weeks the young lion plucked up courage enough to inquire why this was so.

"I know you have the seniority around here, but why do you always get the meat while I get fruit and nuts?" he asked.

"Well," explained the older lion, "this Zoo is so poor that they have only room for one lion, so they have you listed as a monkey."

289. *Alibi*

A teen-ager ordered a "coke" from the drug store soda bar, gulped it down, took a dime out of his pocket, slapped it on the counter and left.

The soda jerk quickly slipped the dime into his pocket, but at the same time, noticed that the store owner had detected his action.

"What a screwy kid," he said nonchalantly to the store

owner, "he comes in, leaves a dime tip ... and walks out without paying!"

290. Special *Delivery*

During World War II a massive flight of Allied bombers set out to spread tons of propaganda leaflets over Germany. All the planes but one returned to base safely. Everyone scanned the skies anxiously as the hours passed without a sign of the missing plane. Finally, the plane came in for a landing two days later. The irate operations officer dashed out and demanded, "Where have you been?"

"Delivering leaflets," said the pilot.

"How long does it take to drop a few leaflets?" asked the officer.

"Drop them?" the pilot exclaimed. "We pushed them under people's doors!"

291. *Welcome* to All

A man took his dog to the veterinarian and asked him to cut his tail off completely.

"I don't like to do that," said the vet. "And why completely?"

"Well," said the dog owner, "my mother-in-law is coming to visit us, and I don't want anything in the house to suggest that she is welcome."

292. Fund-*raising*

At a County Fair the "strong man" was showing his amazing strength. Taking a lemon he squeezed it until the last drop of juice had been removed.

"I will give a hundred dollars to anyone who can squeeze one single drop more from this lemon," he offered.

Several big, husky men tried, but failed in the attempt. A little scrawny individual then up and asked if he could try. To the amazement of everyone, he grasped it in his hand, squeezed it, and juice simply poured out.

"Remarkable," exclaimed the strong man. "How did you do it?"

"Oh, that was simple," said the little man modestly. "You see, I happen to be the treasurer of the First Methodist Church."

293. *Speech* a Little Thin

A young man joined the Peace Corps and was sent to help on a farm. He watched the farmer milk one cow and asked the farmer to let him take over milking the other one.

Sometime later the farmer returned to the barn, just in time to see the young man feeding the milk back to the cow.

"What in the world are you doing that for?" asked the farmer.

The young man explained, "Well, the milk looked a little thin, so I thought I'd run it back through again."

294. The *World* Condition

A lady phoned for her TV serviceman and complained that something was wrong with her set. The serviceman asked if there were any visible symptoms.

"The newscaster is on right now," said the lady, "and he is very long-faced."

"Madam," replied the serviceman, "if you had to report what's happening these days you'd have a long face too!"

295. *Confused*

A farmer was pulling a four-foot rope behind him in his yard. A neighbor asked, "What are you doing with that rope?"

"Well, friend, I've been reading the papers and listening to the radio, and with the world's condition the way it is, I'm so confused that I don't know whether I've lost a cow or found a rope."

296. *Incentive*

A rooster spied a large ostrich egg in the yard next door. He quickly flew over the fence to examine it. He looked it over, kicked it, and stealthily rolled it into his own yard. Then calling all the hens together, he said, "Now, I'm not complaining girls, I'm simply showing you what they are doing in other places."

297. *Speed*

Two golfers were annoyed by an unusually slow twosome in front. One of the offending pair dawdled in the fairway, while the other searched diligently in the rough.

"Why don't you help your friend find his ball?" one of the waiting players shouted indignantly.

"Oh, he's got his ball," the man replied. "He's looking for his club."

298. *Eagerness*

A young man went racing down the ferry slip, and making a tremendous leap, ten feet over the water, he landed with a painful crash on the deck of the Ferry.

As he slowly picked himself up, rubbing his injured side, one of the dockhands sauntered over to him and said quietly: "You didn't have to do that, buddy. This boat is coming in."

Parade

299. *Proud* of Name

A young man made application to change his name according to the provision of the law.

"What's your name?" the judge asked him as he appeared before the Court.

"Bill Stinks, sir," said the applicant.

"Well, I can understand why you want it changed, Bill," said the judge, laughing uproariously.

"And what do you want it changed to?"

"William Stinks, sir," replied the applicant.

300. *Compacts*

The tiny compact car was jerking and jumping, despite the fact that it was on a smooth highway. Finally the driver pulled over to the side of the road.

A sympathetic policeman approached and asked, "Something wrong with the car?"

"No, sir," the driver answered. "It's just that I have the hiccups."

301. *Believe* it or Not

A farmer caught a boy up his apple tree. "Boy, what are you doing up my apple tree?" he asked.

"Well," the little fellow said meekly, "one of your apples fell down, sir, and I'm trying to put it back."

302. *Cost-Plus*

A man came upon a construction crew building a tunnel through a mountain. He said to the construction manager, "I used to do a little construction work myself. We didn't have machinery like you have today, but we had two groups digging, and one would start one way through the tunnel, and the other group on the other side, and we'd meet in the middle."

"Well," the construction manager said, "What if you didn't meet?"

"Well, we would have two tunnels."

Parade

303. *Honesty*

The application blank for a new driver's license held the question, "Have you ever been arrested?"

The applicant put down, "No."

The new question was: "Why?"

The applicant put down, "Never been caught."

304. Taking no *Chances*

A Russian Commissar was so discouraged with life in Moscow that he decided to commit suicide. One evening he walked out to the country, a loaf of bread tucked under his arm. When he came to a train junction, he laid down on the railroad tracks. A peasant passing by was amazed by the strange sight.

"What are you doing," he asked, "lying on these tracks?"

Said the Commissar, "I'm going to commit suicide."

"What do you need the bread for?" asked the peasant.

The Commissar answered, "In this country, by the time the train gets here a man could starve to death."

Parade

305. *Life's Span*

An old legend says that when the Lord created the world, He made men and all the animals to live forty years. The horse forty years, the dog forty years and the monkey forty years.

But man was dissatisfied. He complained that this is not enough time for a man to live. So the horse volunteered ten years of his life to go to the man's life. Then the dog said, "I'll give him ten years of mine too."

Finally, the monkey said, "I'll be a good sport. He can have ten years of mine also."

So, that's the way it is. Man lives his regular forty years —and the next ten he works like a horse—the next ten he leads a dog's life—and the next ten he just monkeys around.

306. *Complaints*

A customer complained to the restaurant manager: "Why do you serve cloudy water in this place?"

The manager was indignant and retorted, "There's nothing wrong with the water sir, the glass is just dirty!"

307. Please Don't *Disturb*

Two Florida beatniks were sitting in the Everglades, dangling their feet in the waters of a swamp. One beatnik exclaimed, "Hey! Daddy! One of them alligators just bit my foot off."

The other one inquired, "Like which one, man?"

The first answered, "What difference does it make, man? If you've seen one alligator, you've seen 'em all."

308. By *Invitation* Only

The conductor on the train discovered that one of the passengers was traveling without a ticket.

"Sir," explained the passenger tearfully, "I am on my way to my daughter's wedding. I have been out of work for months and am 'broke.' "

Deeply moved, the conductor muttered. "That's O.K. buddy. You can ride free if that's the reason."

As he was leaving the compartment the conductor spied another passenger stowed away under the seat.

"And where's your ticket?" he demanded angrily.

"I ain't got one either," explained the little fellow. "You see, I've been invited to the weddin'."

309. Quick *Thinking*

A fellow was trying to skip the military draft and decided to claim faulty vision. The doctor examining his eyes requested that he read the top line on the wall.

"What wall?" asked the draftee.

"My, your sight is bad," the doctor said, and discharged him.

In order to celebrate, the young man took his girl friend to a concert that evening. To his embarrassment, he found the doctor who had examined him sitting in the seat next to him.

"Pardon me, sir," he said, "but does this train go to New York City?"

310. Freedom of *Speech*

Two dogs, one from East and one from West Germany, were discussing the conditions of their different sectors.

"What do you have in the West?" asked the East German dog.

"Oh, I've a heated house, good food, plenty of everything," replied the Western dog. "And what do you have in the East?"

"The food is rotten. We have left-over food and have to sleep in the open . . ." replied the Eastern dog.

"Why do you stay there then?" asked the Western dog.

The Eastern dog replied, "It's just that I like to bark."

311. *Accident Prone*

Harry, one day, attended Sunday school where the class read together the parable of the Prodigal Son, and had a lesson about it.

"And what happened when the prodigal son returned?" asked the teacher when question time came.

"His father went to meet him and hurt himself," replied one of the class, whose name we know.

"Hurt himself?" said the teacher. "Wherever did you learn that?"

"From the Bible, sir," replied Harry. "It says his father ran to meet him and fell on his neck."

312. *Courage*

A small group of weather prophets was on the court-house lawn discussing the weather. They were having quite a time talking about the storms and rains of other days. Weather stories have a way of growing like fish stories.

One man, who was small in stature, remarked that he remembered a time when in that very town it rained nine inches in thirty minutes. There was a moment of silence. Then the town ruffian grabbed him by the shirt and said that he didn't believe it. To prove his disbelief he was going to whip him.

The little man turned to his companion and said, "Sam here remembers it." Sam, being a giant of a man, replied that he did remember the occasion.

The bully grabbed the little man again and said, "Sam may have seen it, but you didn't."

A Bit of Honey

FATHERS—SONS

313. Mistaken *Identity*

A young father, pushing a baby carriage, seemed quite unperturbed by the wails emerging from it. "Easy now, Albert," he said quietly, "control yourself. Keep calm." Another howl rang out. "Now, now, Albert," murmured the parent, "keep your temper."

A young mother passing by remarked, "I must congratulate you." Smilingly she said, "You know just how to talk to babies calmly and gently."

She patted the youngster on the head and cooed, "What's bothering you, Albert?"

"No, no," cried the father, "his name is Harold. I'm Albert."

A Bit of Honey

314. *Endurance*

A young, enthused son said, "Dad, I have my first part as an actor. I play the part of a man that's been married twenty-five years."

"That's a good start, son. Just keep right at it, and one of these days you'll get a speaking part."

315. *Chip* off old *Block*

A little boy was making quite a mess at the table, eating. His father scolded him and said, "Son, you eat like a pig."

Realizing his little boy had never seen a pig, he said, "You do know what a pig is, don't you, son?"

"Yes," the boy replied. "It's a hog's little boy."

316. Only the *Best*

"Dad," said the son of a wealthy man, "can you let me have three hundred dollars to take my girl out to coffee?"

"Three hundred dollars?" asked his dad incredulously. "Where in the world do you take your girl for coffee?"

"Brazil," answered the son, "like any red-blooded American boy."

Parade

317. Women *Drivers*

A young son sadly reported to his dad, "Dad, Mom just backed the car out of the garage and ran over my bicycle."

Father replied, "Serves you right, Son, for leaving it on the front lawn."

318. *Modern* Inventions

First Grader came home one day and told his father, "They've got a magic record player at school."

Father said, "Yes?"

First Grader said, "Yep, you don't need electricity to play it. All you do is wind a crank."

319. *Self-made*

A youngster stood gazing intently at his father's visitor, a homely man of large proportions. At length the portly one, becoming a bit embarrassed, said, "Well, my boy, what are you looking at me for?"

"Why," replied the boy, "Daddy told mother that you were a self-made man and I want to see what you look like."

"Quite right," said the gratified guest. "I am a self-made man."

The boy asked with considerable surprise, "But what did you make yourself like that for?"

320. *Information,* Please

Junior: "Dad, what makes an elephant so big?"
Father: "I don't know."

Junior: "Why is a lion dangerous?"
Father: "I don't know, son."
Junior: "Am I bothering you with my questions?"
Father: "Not at all. You never learn anything if you don't ask."

321. Perfect *Cooperation*

A little old man was near death. His three sons were in the room waiting for the inevitable end. While they were waiting they began to discuss funeral arrangements.

The first son said, "We should have ten cars for the funeral. That way, we'll take care of all the relatives and friends."

The second son said, "Let's just rent two cars and let our relatives follow in their own cars."

The third son said, "Why don't we just rent a station wagon, the three of us get in, and take the casket in beside us?"

At this point, the old man, hearing all this, raised himself from the bed. "Boys," he muttered, "stop arguing. Just get me a pair of pants and I'll walk to the cemetery."

322. *Cheerful* Giver

Hoping to develop his son's character, a father once gave him a penny and a quarter as he was leaving for Sunday school. "Now, Peter, you put whichever one you want in the offering plate," he said.

When the boy returned, his father asked which coin he had given. Peter answered, "Well, just before they sent around the plate the preacher said, 'The Lord loveth a cheerful giver,' and I knew I could give the penny a lot more cheerfully than I could give the quarter, so I gave it."

323. *Pride*

A five-year-old came home every evening complaining that the kids in the neighborhood were picking on him. Finally, the father got hold of the lad one night and showed him a few boxing tricks—how to stand, jab, feint, how to throw his right hand.

"Next time anyone picks on you," he advised, "you let him have it."

Two days later the little boy raced home, ran into the

living room, his eyes ablaze with triumph, his lips parted in a wide smile.

"Dad," he shouted, "I did it. Yes, I did it. I did it. I hit her right in the eye!"

Parade

324. *Comparisons*

Father to his college son, dressed in the latest campus styles: "You look like a fool."

Just then a neighbor approached who obviously was glad to see the boy, saying: "John, you are getting more and more to look like your dad."

Son, dryly: "So father was just telling me."

325. New *Friends*

"Dear Dad," wrote the wandering son. "Here I am in the big city, flat broke, miles away from home and *no friends*. What shall I do?"

The father wired back: "Make some new ones."

HEAVEN

326. *Credit*

A man died and went to heaven. In conversation with St. Peter he asked him how long a minute was in heaven.

St. Peter said, "A million years."

"Well, how much is a penny worth in heaven?" "A million dollars!" he exclaimed.

"Could you lend me a nickel," he asked St. Peter.

"Oh, sure," replied St. Peter, "in a minute."

327. *Surprised* to See You

"How's your wife?" a fellow asked his old friend whom he hadn't seen in some years.

"She's in heaven," replied the friend.

"Oh, I'm sorry," the fellow answered. Then realizing that was not the best phrase to use, he said, "I mean, I'm glad . . . well, what I really mean is, I'm surprised."

328. Not *Anxious*

Uncle Si and Aunt Rose were up in years, but they still

prayed every night. Their prayer was always, "Lord, when you're ready for us, take us. We are ready."

A group of playful boys heard their prayers and decided to have a little fun. They got on top of the house and talked down the chimney . . . in a deep voice . . . "Si—Si!" Aunt Rose asked, "What do you want?"

The voice answered, "I want Si."

"Who are you?"

"I'm from the Lord and I've come for Si."

"Well, he ain't here, he's gone."

"Well, I'll just have to take you, Aunt Rose, instead of Si, if he's not there."

"Get out from under that bed, Si," said Aunt Rose sharply. "You know He knows you are there."

329. *Trustworthy*

A Presbyterian went to heaven and was met by St. Peter. "Where am I permitted to go up here?" he asked.

"Anywhere that you desire," he was told. He looked for a fellow Presbyterian . . . but no Presbyterian. In fact, there didn't seem to be any Presbyterians in heaven.

At last, terribly discouraged, he sought out St. Peter and asked, "Are there no Presbyterians up here?"

"Yes, sure," said St. Peter, and he showed him a big telescope, pointed at the farthest peanut gallery. "There they are, my friend."

"Well, I'm glad they made it. But why are they so far away?"

St. Peter replied: "They are the only ones we can trust so far."

330. *Subject* Matter

A man from Jamestown died and went to heaven. St. Peter was directing the activities and explained, "Each Friday we have a get-together for the new members.

"To break the ice, every new member makes a speech to all the others here, on any subject desired."

"Well," said the man from Jamestown, "I think I'll talk on the Jamestown flood. That was some flood. What do you think of my subject?"

"Well, that's good," said St. Peter, "but I'd better warn you, Noah will be in the audience."

HUSBAND—WIFE

331. *Attention* Wanted

The house next door to the Joneses' seemed to change occupants regularly, so it became the topic of conversation with them. One day, as Mrs. Jones observed the latest neighbor through an upstairs window, she noticed how attentive the new husband was to his wife.

Mrs. Jones reporting this to Mr. Jones said, "Dear, the man next door is so attentive to his wife. He brings her flowers, candy, and kisses her every evening. Now why don't you do that?"

"But dear," Mr. Jones replied, "I hardly know the woman."

332. *Anticipation*

There was a certain woman who was always hearing burglars in the house. One night she called her husband very softly and said, "I tell you, there is someone in this house."

Her husband had heard this complaint many times before. He knew there was no need to argue the case; the quickest way out was to turn on the lights and see. He sleepily crawled out of bed and felt his way into the other room where he turned on the light. To his surprise, there was a burglar with his arms full of things. The burglar immediately dropped the goods and drew a gun on the man of the house. He said, "If you say a word, I'll kill you."

The man, very much awake then, said, "Why, mister, you can keep everything you have, only I would like to make one request of you."

The burglar said, "What is it?"

He replied. "I wish that you would not leave until I run and get my wife. I want her to meet you. She has been looking for you for twenty years."

A Bit of Honey

333. *Authorized*

A group of men was discussing the subject of "Who was boss of the home."

"Who is boss in your home?" one rather hen-pecked member was asked.

"I am boss of my house," he boasted, "and my wife has authorized me to say so."

334. Real *Love*

The long married couple was sitting home watching a television program, when a violent love scene came on the screen.

"Why don't you make love to me like that?" asked the wife, leaning toward him.

"Hey," the husband replied, "do you have any idea how much they pay that fellow?"

335. The Average *Man*

38 around the chest
43 around the waist
98 around the golf course
A nuisance around the house.

336. First *Prize*

Her husband was a heavy snorer and someone suggested, as a remedy, that she tie a ribbon around his nose the next time he snored.

In the early hours of the morning he returned from a meeting, went to bed and began to snore loudly. His wife entered the room, tied a big blue ribbon around his nose, and, much to her relief, he stopped snoring immediately.

The next morning his wife asked, "Where were you last night?"

"I don't remember," he said, suddenly seeing his reflection in the mirror, "but wherever it was, I won first prize."

337. *Shrewd*

An auto on the freeway was speeding at 90 miles an hour. The brakes wouldn't hold, so the woman driver screamed at her husband,

"What should I do? What should I do?"

Said the husband calmly, "Hit something cheap."

338. *Stipulations*

An ardent golfer was on the putting green, when suddenly a woman came running up the fairway, with her wedding gown flying.

"How could you do this to me?"

"Listen," he said, "I told you, *only* if it rained."

339. *Extravagance*

After a big family quarrel, the next morning at the table the husband kept waving a paper in the air and yelling: "You and your suicide attempts. Just look at this gas bill!"

340. *Inequalities*

The widow was crying over a container of ashes. "He was my fourth husband," she wailed.

"Life just isn't fair," an elderly spinster was heard to remark. "She's got husbands to burn, and I can't even get *one*."

341. Something *New* ✕

A housewife called the Sanitary Department to pick up a dead mule in front of her house.

The Department sent several men and a truck, but suddenly she changed her mind. She asked the men to take the mule upstairs and put it in the bathtub. "I'll give you $10 each for doing it," she said.

They didn't understand it, but after all, ten dollars is ten dollars, and so up to the bathroom it went. Afterward they asked: "Why, ma'am, did you want the mule in the bathtub?"

"Well," she said, "my husband has come home every night for thirty-five years and pulled off his coat and shoes, grabbed the newspaper, sat down in his easy chair, and said, 'What's new?' So, tonight, I'm going to tell him."

342. *Endorsement*

A newlywed took her husband's first paycheck to a local bank. The teller looked at the paycheck, then said, "I'm sorry, this check requires an endorsement."

The girl smiled. "I'll have it for you in a moment," she said.

She walked over to a nearby desk and on the back of the check wrote: "My husband, Al McGowan, is one of the kindest men in the world."

343. It's *Later* Than You Think

An old couple had a grandfather clock that struck each hour. Something went wrong with it one day, and it struck eight when it should have struck four . . . and four when it should have struck eight, etc.

That night about eleven o'clock, it really went on a rampage and struck sixteen.

The old man jumped out of bed, shook his wife, and said, "Wake up, old lady, get up quick, it's later than it's ever been before."

344. Modern *Marriage*

"Is your married life a happy one?"

"Yes, I married the woman of my dreams. She is as beautiful to me as the day I met her. Her hands are always white and soft. Her hair is never untidy, and her dresses are always the latest."

"So, you don't regret it?"

"No, but I'm getting pretty tired of eating in restaurants."

345. Modern *Convenience*

"I try to do everything to make my wife happy. She complained about the housework, so I bought her an electric iron, an electric dishwasher and an electric dryer. Then she complained there were so many gadgets around the house that she had no room to sit down . . . so what could I do?"

"Buy her an electric chair!"

346. Having the *Last* Word

The widow expected to inherit all her late husband's wealth. Instead, she learned from the lawyer that her husband had left her five dollars. Everything else went to his secretary.

Naturally, the widow was furious. She drove to the tombstone establishment and summarily ordered the inscription on her husband's monument changed.

"I'm sorry," said the chiseler. "You told me to inscribe 'Rest in Peace' on the stone and that's what I did. I can't change it now, unless you want to buy a new stone."

The widow thought for a moment, then said, "Right

after the words 'Rest in Peace,' you just chisel in, 'Till we meet again.' "

Parade

347. *Unity*

An old man wanted to get an insurance policy. He was examined and during the examination, the doctor asked how old he was. "Seventy-eight," he replied.

"That's too old for a policy, sir, but you are a perfect specimen at your age; how do you account for this?" asked the doctor.

"Well, when we got married we decided that when my wife got mad she would go to the kitchen, and when I got mad I would go outside."

"Yes sir," the old man said enthusiastically, "the outdoors sure agrees with me."

348. *Duel* Life

John had caught some beautiful speckled trout, and, at his wife's suggestion, took some of them to his pastor who lived in the city.

On the way he stopped at the village store to secure some ice for the fish. While he was talking with the storekeeper, a not too honest assistant slipped out the trout and switched some overripe codfish.

You can imagine John's embarrassment as he opened the package when he got to the preacher's house. *What is my wife trying to do to me?* he thought. *Wait till I get her!*

Stopping at the same general store on the way back, he was seen by the assistant, who, sensing something was wrong, quickly and secretly exchanged the cod for the speckled trout once again.

"What's the matter with you? What do you mean?" John asked his wife upon reaching home. "Why did you put rotten codfish in the basket for the pastor?"

"Now, wait a minute," protested his wife. "Let's open the basket and see."

As they opened the basket and saw the trout inside, John shook his head in amazement. "Well," said he, "you may be a speckled trout in the country, but you sure are rotten cod in the city."

349. *Comparisons*

"My wife gets after me about my English. I can speak as well as she can—as a matter of fact, 'weller.' "

350. Gift of *Gab*

The television poll-taker asked: "Do you have your television set on, sir?"

"Yes," replied the man.

"Are other members of your family with you?" the pollster continued.

"Yes, my wife is here."

"To whom are you listening, sir?'

"My wife."

351. In *Name* Only

A wife complained to her husband: "Look at the old clothes I have to wear. If anyone came to visit they would think I was the cook."

The husband replied: "Well, they'd change their minds if they stayed for dinner."

352. *Principles*

When William died suddenly the neighbors were shocked. A kindly woman proceeded to comfort William's wife by describing his good points.

"He was such a man of principle," said the neighbor.

"I know it," said the bereaved woman. "Every Saturday night he'd come home and place his pay envelope in front of me as regular as clockwork. Not a week did he miss, all the time we were married.

"Of course, the envelope was always empty, but look at the principle of the thing."

353. *Self Justification*

A man was walking with his wife and they stopped in front of a drug store to weigh.

"What? Are you overweight, dear?"

"No," she gasped, "but according to this chart I should be six inches taller."

354. Where Least *Expected*

"For months," said the gadabout, "I couldn't discover where my husband spent his evenings."

"And then what happened?" asked a friend.

"Well, one evening I went home and there he was."

355. The *Final* Straw

A business man went to his service club for luncheon, and heard the visiting speaker give a discourse on "Married Life."

Realizing that he had been neglecting his wife, he called his secretary and asked her to buy three dozen red roses and a box of candy. Returning home that evening he kissed his wife, gave her the candy and flowers and greeted her with a big smile.

She began to sob bitterly. "Oh, it's terrible!" she cried. "The baby broke his finger, the Fuller Brush man was here and kept me thirty minutes, the dinner burned, the sink stopped up . . . and now you come home drunk!"

356. The American *Dream*

A refugee couple arrived in the United States several years ago with one dream—to become citizens. Through much red tape and years of study, they were patient and hopeful. Then one day, the husband rushed into the kitchen with the long-awaited news. "Anna! Anna!" he shouted. "At last! We are Americans!"

"Fine," replied the wife, tying her apron around him. "Now you can wash the dishes."

357. *Courtesy*

A Mexican was riding a little mule and his wife was walking behind him.

"Friend, why is your wife not riding?" inquired a visitor.

The Mexican replied, "She ain't got no mule."

358. *Kindly* Word

Husband: "You are just too generous with your kindness. I believe you would have a good word for the devil, himself."

Wife: "Well, he's a very industrious body."

359. *Culinary* Art

A new bride said to her new husband at the first meal

she cooked, "Dear, my mother taught me to cook and I can cook two things well, lemon pie and beef stew."

The husband, biting into the stew, said, "Fine dear, and which is this?"

360. At *Convenient* Time

The wife kept complaining about her husband's nasty temper.

"He's made me such a nervous wreck," the wife complained, "I'm losing weight."

"If that's the case," said her lawyer, "why don't we sue for divorce right now?"

"Let's wait," suggested the wife, "until I'm down to 118."

Parade

KNOWLEDGE—WISDOM

361. *Collection*

A rookie policeman was asked the following question on his examination paper:

"How would you go about dispersing a crowd?"

He answered: "Take up an offering. That will do it every time."

362. *Highway* Driving

Sing while you drive.

At 45 miles per hour sing:

"Highways Are Happy Ways.'

At 55 miles, sing:

"I'm But a stranger Here, Heaven Is My Home."

At 65 miles, sing:

"Nearer My God to Thee!"

At 75 miles, sing:

"When the Roll Is Called Up Yonder I'll Be There."

At 85 miles, sing:

"Lord, I'm Coming Home."

363. *Condolence*

A father was examining his son's report card. "One thing

is definitely in your favor," he announced. "With this report card, you couldn't possibly be cheating."

364. *Lost*

A traveler inquired the way to the post office from a "not too bright" local inhabitant.

"Well, you go down two blocks and turn right ... no, you go down two blocks and turn left ... no, that ain't right either, you go up this street one block, turn right and go one block ... truth is, mister, I don't think you can get to the post office from here at all."

365. *Looks Are Deceiving*

A newspaper interviewed a grizzled old man, sitting with his hands folded in his lap, behind his farmhouse.

"Sir, I'd like to know the secret of your long life," asked the reporter.

"I drink a gallon of whisky, smoke fifty cigars and go out dancing every day of my life," said the man.

"Remarkable!" said the reporter, "and exactly how old are you?"

"Twenty-seven," was the reply.

Parade

366. **Know Where We're *Going***

The pet shop delivery boy was not exactly the brightest lad in the world. One day he was asked to deliver a pet rabbit to "Mrs. Jones, Route 2—Box 4. . . ."

"You had better write that down in case I forget it," said the boy.

Slipping the address into his pocket he started off on his errand. Every few minutes he glanced at the address and said, "I know where I'm going. Mrs. Jones, Route 2—Box 4."

Everything went smoothly until he hit a crater in the road. The truck he was driving landed in a ditch and the rabbit began to run for its life across an open field.

The boy stood there laughing uproariously. When asked by a passer-by what was so funny, he said: "Did you see that crazy rabbit running across that field? He doesn't know where he's going 'cause I've got the address in my pocket."

367. *Curiosity*

A man put his hand in the mule's mouth to see how many teeth the mule had. And the mule closed his mouth to see how many fingers the man had.

Thus the curiosity of both man and mule were satisfied.

368. *Women's* World

This is not a man's world. When he is born they say, "How is the mother?" When he is married, they say, "Isn't she a lovely bride?" When he dies, they say, "How much did he leave her?"

369. *Unity*

A guard in an insane asylum was taking a group of twelve patients out for a walk. They were all big husky men, and the guard was unarmed.

A friend said to him, "John, you should not go out alone with those twelve men. Suppose they should all unite and jump on you at the same time!"

The guard smiled and said, "Unite? Why, don't you know crazy people never unite on anything?"

370. No *Partiality*

The country youth was being examined by the school board. Among the questions asked was: "Do you think the world is round or flat?"

"Well," said the prospective teacher, as he scratched his head in deep thought, "some people think one way and some another, and I'll teach round or flat, just as the parents please."

F'r Instance

371. In *Common*

The guide was showing the tourists the sights of Italy. He said, "Now, here is the Leaning Tower of Pisa."

A deaf tourist said, "I didn't get the name."

The guide repeated, "This is the Leaning Tower of Pisa."

The tourist answered, "I still don't recognize the name,

but it looks like the work of the contractor who built my garage."

372. *Cutting* Corners

The following story is an illustration of how to make burdens easier. Many years ago, two monks were required to do penance and ordered to wear dried peas in their shoes.

One of them walked around limping, while the other walked with ease.

"How can you stand it, walking around so easily on hard, dried peas?" the suffering monk asked his brother.

"Easy," replied the other one, "I boiled them."

373. *Consolation* Prize

The loudspeaker of the big jet clicked on and the captain's voice announced: "Now, there's no cause for alarm, but we felt that you passengers should know that for the last three hours we've been flying without the benefit of radio, compass, radar or navigational beam. This means, in the broad sense of the word, that I am not quite sure in which direction we are heading. I'm sure you'll be interested to know however, on the brighter side of the picture, that we are making excellent time."

374. *Results*

The agent who led his company with persistency in life insurance sales made up his mind he was going to marry the company vice-president's daughter. She didn't like the guy at all, but he knew how to be persistent.

He began an extensive direct mail campaign, supplemented by several phone calls and face-to-face interviews. Soon, he stepped up his direct mail program, sending her a special delivery letter for 47 days. On the 48th day, his persistence produced results.

She married the mailman.

375. *Advertising* Pays

A motorist was driving along a country road when he saw a big sign—"BEWARE OF THE DOG." Farther down the road was another sign—"BEWARE OF THE DOG."

Finally he arrived at the farmhouse and there was a little poodle standing in front of the house.

"Do you mean to say," asked the motorist, "that little dog keeps strangers away?"

"No," replied the farmer, "but the signs do."

376. Sacrifice

A pig and a chicken were going down the street, and were arguing which had contributed the most to society.

They came to a restaurant and the pig said, as he saw the sign, "Ham and eggs"—"See, *you* give out of your abundance, and for me it's a real sacrifice."

377. Worth It All

During World War II a General and a young Lieutenant boarded a train in Europe. With them in the same compartment was a lovely young lady and her maiden aunt. Soon they entered a dark tunnel, and suddenly they heard a kiss and a . . . slap and then came daylight once more.

The General, very red in the face, thought to himself, *The young lady must have tried to hit the Lieutenant, but instead she slapped me!*

The maiden aunt thought to herself, *Ah, I'm glad she had the courage to give him what he deserved.*

The young lady thought, *I'll bet he thought he was kissing me and kissed her instead.*

The young Lieutenant leaned back thinking, *Isn't this a great country! Where else could I kiss the back of my hand, slug a General and get away with it!*

378. Stop Me If You Have Heard It

An inmate of an asylum was observed sitting under a tree in a corner of the grounds. Occasionally his lips would move, then he would laugh hilariously.

This went on for several minutes, then he remained silent.

"What's that man doing?" asked an interested spectator.

"Oh," replied the attendant, "he's telling himself jokes."

"I notice he didn't laugh at the last one he told," said the observer. "How do you explain that?"

"Simple," the attendant replied. "That was one he'd heard before."

379. Not So *Dumb*

A half-wit and a bright boy were seated next to each other at the station.

"Let's play a game of riddles," said the bright boy.

"O.K.," said the half-wit. "How do you play it?"

"Oh, it's easy," explained the other. "You tell a riddle and if I can't answer it, I'll give you a dollar—and vice-versa."

"Well, I'm not as smart as you," the half-wit said, "so I think you ought to give me a dollar if you can't answer, and I give you fifty cents if I can't answer."

"Agreed," said the lad of superior intelligence. "You go first."

"What is it that has four legs, two of them in the air, and thirteen eyes?" asked the half-wit.

The bright boy pondered the question, and giving up in despair, handed over a dollar.

"I give up. What is it?"

"I don't know either," said the half-wit, "and here's your fifty cents."

380. The *Know How*

The inmates of a prison had a joke book they all had memorized. The way they recited them was by the number of the joke. Some fellow would call out a number from one to one hundred, and all would laugh.

A new man in the prison, after studying the book, said he wanted to tell a joke. They said, "O.K., shoot!"

He said, "Number 20" ... but nobody laughed. He said, "This is funny. What's wrong, why aren't you laughing?"

A fellow nearby said, "Some can tell them and some can't."

381. *Flowers* to the Living

Years ago in the Hawaiian Islands, the Chinese had this custom: When a friend or relative died, they would bury him, then place a nine course dinner on his grave to feed his spirit.

On one occasion, an American went into a cemetery to place flowers on the grave of a pal. While doing so he spotted a Chinese mourner at a nearby grave setting out the usual nine course meal for the spirit of the departed friend.

The American, thinking this a rather wasteful and ridiculous custom, mockingly inquired, "When do you think your friend will come up and eat his food?"

The Chinese smiled, "Same time," he answered, "your friend come up and smell your flowers."

Parade

382. *Diets*

Everyone you talk to these days is on a diet. Well, I've got one that really works. The first day you cut out meat ... the second day you cut out starches ... the third day you cut out liquids ... and the fourth day you cut out paper dolls!

* * *

A diet specialist said to a lady, "Now if you will follow my directions, I guarantee you will lose weight, and you can eat anything you want."

"You mean eat anything I want?"

"Yes," he replied, "but don't swallow."

383. Good to be *Wanted*

The ex-con saw his picture posted on the bulletin board of the post office. He turned to a buddy and said proudly: "Ain't it good to be wanted?"

384. In *Doubt*

A lady wrote to the "Dear Abby" column in a newspaper ... she said: "I have been engaged to a man for some time, but just before the wedding, I find he has a wooden leg. Do you think I should break it off?"

385. *Hot* Weather

A tourist was looking for a certain location and inquired the way from a local farmer. The farmer explained that he was not good in giving directions, but would be happy to ride over with the motorist to show him the way.

The farmer traveled in the tourist's air-conditioned Cadillac, the distance of several miles to the destination and was returned to the farm afterwards by a grateful motorist.

"Zeke, what are you going to do for the rest of the day?" inquired the farmer's wife.

"Well, I was goin' to do some grubbin', but it's turned off so durned cold, I think I'll kill hogs," the farmer replied.

LAW

386. Eye For Business

A shrewd and thrifty farmer got into a dispute with a neighbor over a boundary line. The battle raged, and agreement seemed impossible.

At last he consulted a lawyer, who agreed if there were no grounds for suit, he would make no charge for his services. The farmer outlined the case. After hearing it, the lawyer declared, "Yes, there are grounds for suit. It will cost you a hundred dollars, so if you give me just fifty dollars as a retainer, I will proceed."

"No," said the thrifty farmer. "I guess I'll not go ahead with it, for I just gave you the other fellow's side."

387. Professional *Dexterity*

The family lawyer had been called upon to trace back the ancestry of illustrious New England aristocrats.

After months of careful research he discovered that one member of the family had been hanged for sheep stealing, sometime in the 1800's. Not wanting to embarrass the family, he sent them this report: "John was standing on a platform when it suddenly gave way."

388. Practical *Advice*

One of the greatest criminal lawyers in the nation recently got an urgent phone call from one of his clients.

Said the client to the lawyer, "I'm in prison, and they've shaved my head, transferred me to death row, cut a slit in my trousers. What should I do?"

Said the lawyer, "Don't sit down."

Parade

389. *Thought* Needed

Two insurance company lawyers were conducting a trial against a woman suing their company for damages. The plaintiff had only one lawyer, and it seemed that the two lawyers for the defense, both brilliant and elegant, were really getting the better of the case.

"Don't you think you had better get another lawyer to help you?" suggested the plaintiff to her lawyer.

"Why?" he asked.

"Well," she observed. "I noticed that when one of those lawyers are talking, the other is thinking, but when you are talking, nobody is thinking."

390. *Jury*

A new attorney, representing his first client, was suing a man for killing twenty-four hogs.

Trying to make an impression, he said to the jury:

"Twenty-four hogs, gentlemen, twenty-four. Twice the number that's here in the jury box."

391. *Stubborn*

The jury had spent many hours in fruitless wrangling without reaching a verdict. Finally the foreman sent out a note to the waiting Judge: "Please send us eleven dinners and a bag of oats."

392. *Criminal* Lawyer

A stranger entered a small midwestern town and asked one of the men on the street, "I am looking for a criminal lawyer; have you one in your town?"

"Well," said the native, "we're pretty sure we have, but we can't prove it."

A Bit of Honey

393. *Revenge*

Two lawyer friends were caught speeding and were brought before the Judge. The Judge said, "Now, you two lawyers are qualified, so I am going to allow you to try each other's case."

The first acting Judge said to his friend, "You were doing 50 miles per hour in a fifteen mile zone ... how do you plead?"

"I plead guilty," he replied.

"All right, I fine you $25.00," and his friend paid his fine.

He then became acting Judge and said, "You are charged with going fifty miles per hour in a fifteen mile zone . . . how do you plead?"

"Guilty."

"That will be $50.00. This is the second case of this type today."

LOGIC—REASONING

394. Weather *Prognosticator*

A tourist stopped at a combination service station and general store in the country.

An old man was basking in the sun, holding a short piece of rope.

"What's the rope for, sir?" the tourist asked.

"It's a weather gauge," replied the old man.

Puzzled, the tourist asked, "How can a piece of rope tell the weather?"

"Simple, sonny," said the old man. "When it swings back and forth the wind is blowing. When it gets wet it's raining."

395. *Cynicism*

Isaac was an old Negro who had an old ferryboat on the Red River. One day a white man asked him, "Uncle Isaac, I haven't any money, but I wish you would row me across the river."

Uncle Isaac looked this man over and then said, "Boss, if you ain't got no money, it don't make no diffunce which side ob de river youse on."

A Bit of Honey

396. *Expert*

A fellow had two parrots and he wanted to know which was the male and which was the female. A man standing near said, "I am a bird expert, and I can tell you."

"If you will notice every time the birds eat worms, the

male bird always eats the male worms and the female bird eats the female worms."

"Well, how do you know which is the male and which is the female worm?"

"Well, I don't know that. I'm just a bird expert."

397. *Holding Own*

The weary traveler inquired of a passerby, "How far is it to Dublin?"

"Just down the road, first on the right about five miles and you're there," the stranger said helpfully.

Some three hours later, after walking without a pause, he came upon another stranger. "How far is it to Dublin?" he inquired again.

"Oh, just about five miles in that direction," came the reply.

"Well," said the weary traveler, as he ambled on, "at least I'm not losing any distance."

398. *Out of Season*

John had been convicted of highway robbery in Alabama and sentenced to death. The last day of his life had come. The warden awakened him and asked him what he would have for breakfast. "As it is your last day, John, you can have anything you want."

"Thank you, boss, I reckon I'll just take watermelon."

"But this is December! Watermelons aren't planted yet, much less ripe!"

"Never mind, boss. I can wait."

399. Time to *Talk*

Two old maids boarded a jet plane. On the plane, one said to the other, "Do you know this plane travels faster than sound?"

The other was quite alarmed about this and when they were settled she said to the captain: "I beg your pardon, sir, but does this plane travel faster than sound?"

Proudly he said, "Yes, ma'am, we fly faster than sound."

"Well," replied the lady, "please slow it down a little, for my friend and I want to talk."

400. It's a *Long* Distance

The new maid answered the phone, "Yes, you are right," she said, and hung up the receiver.

Again the phone rang and she answered, "Yes, ma'am, it sure is!" and hung up again.

"Who was that?" asked her mistress.

"I don't know, ma'am," replied the maid. "Some crazy lady kept saying, "It's a long distance from New York," and I said, "It sure is."

401. The *Thin* Line

A motorist had a flat tire in front of the insane asylum. He took the wheel off, and the bolts that held the wheel on, rolled down into the sewer.

An inmate, looking through the fence, suggested that the man take one bolt from the remaining three wheels to hold the fourth wheel in place until he could get to the service station.

The motorist thanked him profusely and said, "I don't know why you are in that place."

The inmate said, "I'm here for being crazy, not for being stupid."

402. *Companionship*

A man was walking down the main street of a small town, with a dog on a leash. It was a miserable looking, flea-bitten, mangy, purple-eyed pup.

"Where are you going with that 'mutt'?" a friend asked.

"Oh, I'm taking him to the New York Dog Show."

"That flea-bitten, mangy, purple-eyed character? You know you'll never win a prize, don't you?"

"Yes, I know," he replied, "but it will give him a chance to meet a lot of mighty fine dogs."

403. *Comparisons*

A cynical professor told his class that if any of them could answer his one question he would allow that individual to forego the regular examination. The question was: "If a boat floats five miles downstream while a crow flies eight miles across an open field in the same time that a sparrow flies ten and a half miles counterclockwise, then how old am I?"

"You are forty-four years old, sir," answered one of the pupils.

"Remarkable," exclaimed the professor. "Tell me, exactly how did you arrive at that figure?"

"That was easy, sir," replied the student modestly. "You see, I have a nephew who's twenty-two, and he's only *half crazy*."

404. *Transportation* Needed

An intoxicated fellow staggered out of the hotel, walked up to a man in uniform and said, "Call me a cab."

"I beg your pardon," said the man in uniform, "I happen to be an Admiral in the United States Navy."

"All right then, Admiral," said the inebriate, "call me a boat."

Parade

405. Wrong *Direction*

The passenger in the taxi cab was more than slightly inebriated. Glancing at his watch he saw that the time was seven o'clock. Shortly afterward he glanced at a clock in a jeweler's store which registered 6:55.

"Hey, what's the time?" he asked the cabbie.

"It's 6:50," the cabbie replied.

"Stop and turn around," he demanded, "we're going in the wrong direction!"

406. Young *Love*

The English professor at school, over and over again, emphasized the importance of developing an extensive vocabulary.

"You have my assurance," he told the class, "that if you repeat a word eight or ten times, it will be yours for life."

In the rear row, an attractive co-ed sighed, and closing her blue eyes, muttered softly to herself, "Steve—Steve—Steve."

Parade

407. Getting *Up* in the World

A very disturbed individual got on a double decker bus for the first time, in a large city. After bothering the driver for several minutes he took the driver's advice and went up on the next deck.

Soon he came down again, and the driver asked, "Why didn't you stay up on the other deck?"

"Do you think I'm crazy?" the fellow asked. "There's no driver up there."

408. Great *Discovery*

Ivenson, the Swede, was late for work every morning. At last the patience of the boss ran out.

"Listen, Ivenson, if you're late one more time you're fired," his boss told him.

Realizing it was because his alarm clock was not working, he proceeded to pull it apart, when out fell a dead cockroach.

Ivenson exclaimed, "Ah, dat's de trouble! No vonder she von't run, the engineer she is dead!"

409. *Results* Count

A city miss asked an old farmer: "Which is correct grammatically, sir, to say a hen is 'setting' or 'sitting'?"

The farmer replied: "I don't know miss, and it don't interest me at all. What I wonder, when I hear a hen cackle, is if she's 'laying' or 'lying.'"

410. *Family* Tree

The old man was telling about his family. "The first one is a doctor ... the second one stays out all night too ... the third one is a lawyer, and the fourth one won't tell the truth either. The fifth one is a school teacher ... and the sixth one is always broke too ... The seventh one is a preacher ... and the eighth one ... well, he won't work either."

411. *Catching* On

All day long the asylum inmate busily pushed a wheel-barrow around the grounds upside down.

Finally, one of the attendants said to him: "That's no way to push a wheelbarrow. Turn it right side up when you push it."

The inmate replied, "I did at first, but they kept putting bricks in it."

412. *Marksmanship*

After the rifle tournament was completed, one young army recruit was very discouraged by his poor showing. As he turned in his card to the top sergeant, he remarked, "What a score! I feel like shooting myself!"

"Well," replied the sergeant sympathetically, after looking over the card, "you'd better take two bullets."

Parade

413. Playing *Safe*

George wasn't any too bright, and the gang liked to pick on him. One day they showed him a huge watermelon and bet him fifty cents he couldn't eat it all at one session. Before venturing, however, George hurried home, returning some fifteen minutes later, and proceeded to demolish the whole melon without stopping.

"Why did you go home first, George?" they asked him.

"Mom had a bigger melon in the kitchen, and I knew if I could eat it, I could eat this smaller one."

414. Good *Reason*

Caller: "Long distance. I want to place a call to Damariscota, Maine."

Telephone operator: "How do you spell that please?"

Caller: "Listen, lady, if I could spell it I'd write."

MONEY—WEALTH

415. Young *Finance*

A kid moved to El Paso from Houston and pledged $100 a week to the Methodist Church. The pastor thought this 10-year-old was fooling, so he called up the boy's father and told him about the pledge the kid had signed.

"That's quite all right," the father said. "We believe firmly that Tommy should tithe his weekly income. He's in oil, you know."

416. *Dumb*-Bills

A counterfeiter made a mistake and turned out a number of bills of a $15 denomination. Not wanting to throw the spurious bills away, he decided to try to pass them off on a hillbilly.

"Say, buddy, can you give me change for a fifteen dollar bill?" he asked.

"Sure can!" said the hillbilly, as he handed him two six-dollar bills and one three-dollar bill.

417. *Inflation*

Every day for six months the businessman walked past the corner beggar and dropped ten cents in the beggar's box. But, being a charitable fellow, the businessman never took any shoe laces out of the box. One day when he had dropped his usual dime, the businessman felt the beggar's hand on his arm. He noticed the fellow was about to say something.

"Yes," said the businessman, without waiting for the question, "I suppose you are wondering why I never take shoelaces after I put my dime in the box."

"No," said the beggar, "I just wanted to tell you that the price of shoelaces is going up to fifteen cents next week."

Parade

418. "E" For *Effort*

At an auction, the selling was halted briefly when the auctioneer raised his hand and announced, "A gentleman in the room has just lost a wallet containing $1,000. For it's immediate return, he is offering a reward of $250."

There was a brief silence. Then from the back was heard, "$255?"

419. Great *Generosity*

The beggar was dirty and hungry and as the old lady passed by she gave him five cents. She said, "Tell me, how did you get so destitute?"

"Well, ma'am," the old beggar said, "I was like you at one time, always giving vast sums to the poor."

420. Perfect *Trust*

A man got a haircut but didn't have the money to pay for it. The barber said, "We don't do credit work here, but you can sign an I-O-U and we will put it on the wall with the others who owe me."

"But, I object to having it on the wall. I don't want anyone to see my name."

"They won't see it, brother, your coat will be hanging over it."

421. Working *Together*

Thieves were robbing a house when suddenly a chair was knocked over. The man of the house was awakened and he jumped out of bed and said, "What are you looking for?"

"Money," the robber replied.

"Well, turn on the light and I'll help you look."

422. *Rank and File*

A well-known rich man approached his 7-year-old son and said, "I'm sorry, son, but tomorrow morning I have to use the chauffeur and limousine for business."

"But Daddy," objected the 7-year-old, "how will I get to school?"

"You'll get to school like every other kid in America," answered the father angrily. "You'll take a cab!"

Parade

423. *Poverty*

In Hollywood, there is an exclusive school attended by children of movie stars, producers and directors. Asked to write a composition on the subject of poverty, one little girl started her literary piece: "Once there was a poor little girl. Her father was poor, her mother was poor, her governess was poor, her chauffeur was poor, her butler was poor. In fact, everybody in the house was very, very poor."

424. *Honesty*

An old miser, because of his exceptional thrift, had no friends. Just before he died, he called his doctor, lawyer, and minister together around his bedside.

"I have always heard that you can't take it with you, but I am going to prove you can," he said. "I have $90,000 in cash under my mattress. It's in three envelopes of $30,000 each. When I pass on I want each of you to take an envelope and just before they throw the dirt on me, you throw your envelope in."

The three attended the funeral and each threw his envelope in the grave. On the way back from the cemetery the minister said, "I just don't feel exactly right. My conscience hurts me. I'm going to confess. I needed $10,000 badly for a new church we are building, so I took out $10,000 and threw the $20,000 in the grave."

The doctor said, "I too, must confess, I am building a hospital and I took $20,000, and threw in only $10,000.

The lawyer said, "Gentlemen, I'm surprised, shocked and ashamed of you. I don't see how you could hold out like this. I threw in my personal check for the full amount."

425. Secret of *Success*

A millionaire was asked how he got rich.

"Well," he said, "I began by buying peanuts for five cents a bag and selling them for ten cents. I worked long hours and all holidays. However, I didn't become a millionaire for another five years."

"What happened?" his interviewer asked.

"Well, then my father died and left me a chain of hotels."

426. True *Love*

Did you hear the heart-warming story about the boy who was born on the East Side of New York of poverty stricken immigrant parents? He grew up and married a neighborhood girl and had several children. For years he struggled, but all of a sudden everything changed. He became tremendously wealthy. He owned steel mills, oil refineries, railroads. He had a home in Miami, a villa on the Riviera, an estate in Rome. But he never forgot.

Every year he goes back to the lower East Side, just to visit his wife and children.

427. *Appreciation*

A Texan "got very rich quickly" when oil was discovered on his ranch. He bought a lavish white Cadillac, with every gadget on it that could be bought. He drove furiously about the community advertising his wealth.

Then one day he fell ill. It was evident that he would not

recover. Before his death he asked that he be buried in his white Cadillac. A great hole was dug in the cemetery, and a large crane lowered the Cadillac into the grave, with the dead man laid out on its large back seat.

As to the strange coffin lowered into the grave, a man in the watching crowd was heard to say, "Man! that's really living!"

Holiday Inn

428. A Sense of *Values*

The lawyer gathered the family of the recently deceased Sam Wong Berg around him.

He began to read Sam's will aloud: "To my dear wife, I leave my house, fifty acres of land and one million dollars."

"To my son, Sam, I leave my two cars and $100,000."

"To my daughter, Bessie, I leave my yacht and $100,000."

"And to my brother-in-law, who always insisted that health is better than wealth, I leave my sun lamp."

Parade

429. Full *Vision*

A hitchhiker, thumbing a ride from Dallas to Fort Worth, was picked up by a big limousine. As the car sped along, the hitchhiker noticed a pair of spectacles, with extremely thick lenses, on the seat next to the driver.

Feeling anxious about the tremendous speed they were traveling, he leaned over and said politely to the driver, "Excuse me, sir, but I think you forgot to put your glasses on."

"Forget it, son," said the Texan. "You see the windshield on this car? It's ground to my prescription."

Parade

430. Not Always *Quantity*

A Texan, on the plane, began bragging of the property he owned.

"How much property do you own?" asked the man seated next to him.

"Thirty acres," answered the Texan.

"That doesn't sound like much for a Texan," said the other fellow.

"Downtown Dallas," he retorted.

Parade

431. Taking No *Chance*

A rich Texan suddenly clutched his heart, then yelled at his wife: "I think I'm gonna have an attack. Well, don't just stand there, girl. Buy me a hospital!"

Parade

432. Taking A *Chance*

A Texas oil man visited the dentist for a checkup.

The dentist examined his teeth and said, "Not a cavity—they are all perfect."

The oil man said, "Drill anyway—I feel lucky today."

MOTHERS—DAUGHTERS

433. Vivid *Imagination*

The late G. Campbell Morgan related this story of his granddaughter, Penelope, a precocious child, who later became a radiant Christian worker and witness.

One day Penelope rushed indoors shouting, "Oh, Mother, there's a big black bear in the backyard!"

"You know perfectly well it's only a big dog," said her mother. "Now go to your room and ask God to forgive you for telling a lie."

"Did you ask God to forgive you?" she asked when Penelope came downstairs a little later.

"Yes," Penelope replied, "and He said it was quite all right. He thought it was a bear Himself when He first saw it."

434. *Part* Payment

Daughter: "Mom, do you love me?"
Mom: "Sure I love you."
Daughter: "How much am I worth to you?"
Mom: "You're worth a million dollars."
Daughter: "Then could you advance me a quarter?"

435. *Quality* Music

Two music editors were yawning over a new manuscript: "I've never heard such corny lyrics, such simpering sentimentality, such repetitious, uninspired melody. Man, we've got a hit on our hands."

A Bit of Honey

436. Above the *Average*

The young bee-bop-bug enthusiast bought every record that made the top ten in the jazz world. One day she 'phoned her local music store, but accidentally dialed the wrong number and got the plumbing company by mistake.

The conversation went something like this: "Hello, do you have 'Ten Little Fingers and Ten Little Toes in Alabama?' "

A deep bass voice on the other end of the line replied, "No ma'am, but I have a wife and thirteen kids in Texas."

"Is that a record?" the young lady asked.

"No, ma'am," the deep voice replied, "but I'm sure it's much above the average."

437. *Compromise*

The soloist was singing in a high-pitched voice, well beyond her vocal range.

She came to the phrase: "He is the fairest of ten thousand," and her voice broke as she came to the "ten."

Undaunted, she tried again, but met with no greater success the second time.

"Give me my note again," she requested of the pianist, and made a frantic third attempt.

"Lady," someone in the audience called, "I don't think you're gonna make it. Don't you think you'd better start over again and try for five thousand this time?"

438. *Practice* Makes Perfect

The Opera Company was far from prosperous and hired an understudy for the leading soloist at a very reasonable rate, hoping sincerely that they would never have to use him. One night the inevitable happened—the leading soloist developed laryngitis, and the understudy had to perform. He sang his number. There was a long pause ... and then a burst of applause. He sang it once more. Again a long silence . . . and a burst of applause.

After this had occurred four times, he said, "Ladies and gentlemen, I will not sing this number again."

A voice from the back of the audience called out, "Yes you will, you bum, you'll keep singing it till you learn it!"

439. No Ear For *Music*

A musician had a theory that animals had a basic, lovable instinct, and could be tamed by music.

To prove it he went to the heart of Africa and began to play lovely melodies on his violin. In amazement the crocodiles came to listen; the elephants joined with them, and a host of other dangerous animals joined the throng, entranced by the plaintive melodies.

Suddenly a lion burst through the group, smashed the violin and devoured the musician.

"What did you do that for?" roared the leopard. "Didn't you like this beautiful music?"

Cupping a front paw to his ear the lion said, *"Eh?"*

440. *Singing*

The would-be singer was quite proud of the fact that someone told him he had a mellow voice.

Then he found the definition of the word "mellow" in the dictionary. It read "over-ripe and almost rotten."

* * *

A man was asked to lead the congregational singing.

"I can't do it," he replied.

"The last time I tried, the piano player said she played on all the black keys—and on all the white keys—and I still sang in the cracks."

NATIONAL BACKGROUND

441. *Closing* Soon

Two Irishmen, Pat and Mike, were sitting under a persimmon tree one day, and Pat became hungry. So he picked up a green persimmon and ate it.

"Mike," he finally said, "do you have anything you want to ask me? 'Cause if you do, you'd better ask it now, for I'm closing up fast."

442. Bring *Visitors*

A plane was crossing the ocean, when suddenly the pilot came to the cabin door and explained there was engine trouble, and that if four people didn't get off the plane to lighten the load, all would perish. He asked for volunteers.

An Englishman came to the back door, knelt, held his nose, and cried, "God save the King," and jumped overboard.

Then a Frenchman came to the back door, knelt, held his nose, cried, "Vi-ve-la France," and jumped out.

Finally a long, lanky Texan took his position at the back door and cried, "Remember the Alamo" ... and pushed two Mexicans overboard.

443. *Late*

Two men got into a hot argument and decided to settle things the way they do in the old country ... with guns.

On the appointed morning, Francois was on hand with his pistol, a second and his physician. After about an hour a messenger arrived with a telegram from Bourveaux.

"Dear Francois:" it read, "If I'm late don't wait for me. Go ahead and shoot."

444. Worthy of *Occasion*

A southern boy accidentally fell into a barrel of molasses while visiting the country store.

Looking up, he said, "Oh, Lord, make my tongue worthy of this occasion."

445. Volunteer

A minister wanted to raise a large sum of money for the building project.

He wired the chairs of ten of his most influential members with an electric current. Then after announcing that he wanted ten volunteers willing to give a thousand dollars each, he pressed the switch.

Nine immediately jumped to their feet. "The result," he

announced, "is nine volunteers standing and one electrocuted Scotsman."

446. Silence Is Golden

An old preacher was about ready to preach one Sunday morning, when suddenly as he looked around, he spied an old cellmate of his in the congregation.

He said, "Brothers and Sisters, I'm going to change my text this morning. I'm taking my text from II Calamity, 3rd chapter . . . "He that seeth and openeth not his mouth, the same will I reward after the service is over."

447. National Pride

A Boston salesman visited Texas and heard one particular Texan boasting about heroes of the Alamo who, alone, held off whole armies.

"I don't think you ever had anyone so brave around Boston," challenged the Texan.

"Did you ever hear of Paul Revere?" asked the Bostonian.

"Paul Revere?" said the Texan. "Isn't that the guy who ran for help?"

448. Same All Over

Six young housewives living in the same apartment building in Canada fell into a dispute of much magnitude that it resulted in their being haled into court. When the case was called, they all made a concerted rush for the bench and, reaching it, all broke bitter complaints at the same moment.

The judge sat momentarily stunned, as charges and countercharges filled the air. Suddenly he rapped for order. When quiet had been restored, the patient magistrate said gently, "Now, I'll hear the oldest first."

That closed the case.

449. Good Business

A salesman had taken a large order from a Scottish manager and endeavored to give him a box of cigars for the order.

"Naw," he replied, "Dinna try to bribe a mon. I couldna tak' them, I am a member of the kirk!"

"But will you accept them as a present?"

"I cudna," said the Scot.

"Well, then," said the salesman, "suppose I sell you the cigars for a small sum—say sixpence?"

"Well, in that case," replied the Scot, "since you press me, and not liking tae refuse an offer weel meant, I think I'll be takin' two boxes."

450. The Kid's Speech

A Methodist missionary to the Spanish mission in Florida was giving a program for the children and had given them pieces to learn. One day he received a note from a mother: "Dear Pastor—I am sorry Carlos will not be able to recite on Friday. The goat ate his speech."

451. No *Waste*

An Englishman, an American, and a Scotchman were dining in a restaurant, when, by some strange happening, a fly fell into each of their bowls of soup.

The Englishman daintily removed the fly with a spoon.

The American casually flipped his out with his finger.

But the Scotchman lifted his fly out and, squeezing it with both hands, cried, "Spit it out—spit it out."

452. *Thriftiness*

A thrifty farmer named Sandy fell into an open well. Almost drowning, he began to tread water and call to his wife for help.

"Hold on," she cried, "I'll call the workmen in from the field to get you out."

"Wait," gasped Sandy. "What time is it?"

"Eleven-thirty," said his wife.

"Wait another half hour," gasped Sandy. "I can swim around till dinner time.

453. *Generosity*

A Scotchman, not too familiar with American ways, was suing for a divorce.

At the trial the judge said to the wife, "I give you $50 per week alimony."

The old Scotchman spoke up and said, "Judge, that's

decent of you, and I'll throw in a couple of bucks weekly myself."

454. *Do-It-Yourself*

A Scotchman went to the dentist and asked, "Doc, how much do you charge to pull a tooth?"

"Five dollars," answered the dentist.

"Well, here's a buck," said the thrifty Scot. "Loosen it!"

Parade

455. *Safety*

An aged couple was listening to a broadcast church service. Both sat in deep contemplation, and half an hour went by. Then suddenly the old man burst into a fit of laughter.

"Sandy," exclaimed his wife in a horrified tone, "why this merriment on the Sabbath?"

"Ah," said Sandy, "the preacher's just announced the offering, and here I am safe at home."

456. Playing It *Safe*

A Scotchman who was taking a train trip alighted at every stop and went into the depot.

A fellow traveler observing this strange behavior, inquired the reason for it.

The Scotchman explained, "I have heart trouble and my doctor says I may drop dead any minute, so I just buy a ticket from station to station."

457. *Strategy*

Three Scotchmen planned to arrive at church late so they would miss the offering.

But, as they came in, a special offering was being taken. Quickly one of them fainted and the other two took him out.

458. Almost *Weakened*

Hymie always wanted to take a plane ride and asked how much the trip was.

"Ten dollars for fifteen minutes," the pilot replied.

"Ten dollars! That's too much," said Hymie.

"I'll tell you what I'll do," said the pilot. "If you and

your wife keep perfectly silent on this trip I'll let you travel free. But if you make one sound I will charge you double —twenty dollars."

Agreed, the couple got in the plane, whereupon the pilot looped the loop, pretended to crash, dive, and went through all kinds of aerial acrobats.

When the plane landed, he shook Hymie's hand.

"You're a good sport," he said. "I don't understand how you were able to keep quiet for all that length of time."

"Well," confessed Hymie, "I did nearly yell out one time when my wife, Mary, fell out."

PATIENCE

459. *Patience*

The angler was exasperated with a fellow who sat by watching him. Finally, he could stand it no longer.

"You've been watching me for three hours. Why don't you try fishing yourself?" he asked testily.

"I ain't got the patience," replied the onlooker, as he continued to just sit and stare.

460. *Popularity*

The sailors were lining up for their discharge from the Navy, and the officer who was stamping the discharge papers said to the boy who was next in line: "Well, Seaman Smith, you never liked me. I suppose you can hardly wait until I die so you can come back and spit on my grave."

The Seaman answered solemnly, "Lieutenant, I'll never stand in line again!"

Parade

461. *Fear* Brings Power

There was a young English boy by the name of Orrie. He was of a home of very meager circumstances. Nights when they didn't have enough food for supper, they resorted to a dish known as "Sparrow Pie." He was met at the back door by his mother one day, and she told him to go for some sparrows for sparrow pie.

The best way to hunt them was to go to a group of trees in a cemetery, late in the evening. He crept carefully up— and was ready to make a mighty sweep with a big stick, when suddenly he fell into a freshly dug grave, as yet unoccupied. He tried to get out, but it had rained and the sides were as slick as glass.

He knew his mother would send someone for him, and she did. His big brother. But just as he got near the grave another terrible thing happened. His brother also fell into the grave. It was dark and he didn't know he was not alone, so he pushed and shoved, but it had rained in his end of the grave as much as in the other end, and the harder he pushed and shoved, the harder he fell to the bottom. Young Orrie had enjoyed the show, but knew that all good things must come to an end, so he decided to make as much of the dramatic situation as possible. He sat up very straight in his end of the grave . . . gathered all the diaphragmic tones well underneath him, and with all the eerie, ghastly tones he could muster, he said, *"Friend, can't you let a man rest in peace?"*

There was a deadening silence in his end of the grave, then something that resembled a rocket zoomed by old Orrie's head, and his brother, who hadn't been able to make six feet to the top of the grave, made twenty feet past it on his first jump.

462. *Will Power*

A lady was approached by a beggar. He said, "I haven't eaten for six days."

The lady said, "Oh, if I had your will power."

Parade

463. *Alibis*

A gentleman came to an office and asked to speak to Mr. Smith.

"I'm sorry," the secretary told the fellow, "but Mr. Smith can't see you today. He has a sprained back."

"Well," replied the visitor, "tell Mr. Smith I didn't come here to wrestle with him. I just want to talk to him."

POLITICS

464. *Interpretation*

"Political difference is wholesome. It's political indifference that hurts."

An illustration of the fact that it's all in the viewpoint is this conversation:

"Dad, what's a traitor in politics?"

"Well, son, a traitor is a man who deserts our party and goes over to the opposition."

"I see. Well, what's a man who leaves the other party and comes across to yours?"

"That's different, son. He's a convert."

Parade

465. *Confidence*

A wise man once said, "I have a lot of good friends in a certain political party, and I'd trust them anywhere—except in office."

466. *Objective*

A prominent politician, when he was a candidate for an important municipal office, said to three Negroes that he would give a fat turkey to the one who'd give the best reason for being a Republican.

The first one said, "I'se a 'Publican cause de 'Publican sot us darkies free."

"Very good, Peter," said the politician.

"Now, Bill, let me hear from you."

"Well, I'se a 'Publican cause dey done give us de protective tariff."

"Fine," exclaimed the politician.

"Now, Sam, what do you have to say?"

"Boss," said Sam scratching his head and shifting from one foot to the other, "Boss, I'se a 'Publican 'cause I wants that turkey."

467. *Politician*

You can always tell a politician ... but you can't tell him much.

468. Typical *Politician*

When Columbus started out, he didn't know where he was going. When he got there, he didn't know where he was. When he got back, he didn't know where he had been. And he did all of it on other people's money.

What a politician Columbus would have been.

469. Good *Advice*

The politician said to his manager: "As I was shaving this morning I was thinking of my message and cut my face."

The manager replied: "The next time you shave, think of your face and cut your message."

470. Political *Friends*

A well-known politician asked one of the opposition to loan him a dime. "I want to call one of my friends," he explained.

"Here's fifty cents," offered the other. "Take it and call *all* of your friends."

471. *Pleasing* Everybody

A well-known politician was riding in a plane, when he suddenly produced a five dollar bill and said, "I'm going to throw this five dollar bill out the window and make somebody happy."

One of his ardent admirers suggested, "But sir, why don't you throw five one dollar bills out and make five people happy?"

A member of the opposition, seated in the corner, growled, "Why don't you *jump* out yourself and make *everybody* happy!"

472. Sectional *Bias*

A northern political leader purchased what he thought was enough cloth for a new suit, and submitted it to several tailors. But each one reported that it was not enough cloth for a man of his size.

A tailor in the deep south heard about the situation, and volunteered to make the suit. The cloth was sent to him and in a few days he called and asked if he wanted two pairs of pants to the suit, and also pleats in the trousers.

"I don't understand," replied the politician. "The other tailors couldn't make a suit with *one* pair of pants, to say nothing of pleats."

"Well," replied the southern tailor, "you are not nearly as big down South as you are up North."

473. Political *Rewards*

A famous politician was rescued from drowning by three young lads.

"I will give you anything you want," he promised his rescuers gratefully.

"I'll take a bicycle, sir," the first lad said.

"I would like a motor bike," added the second boy.

"Sir, if it's all the same to you, I'd like a military funeral."

"A military funeral! ... Why?" asked the famous politician.

"Because," the boy said, "when my paw finds out whose life I saved, he'll sure kill me!"

474. Vote of *Confidence*

Mr. Khrushchev wanted to find out what people really thought of him. Naturally, they would not tell him if they recognized him, so he dressed in an elaborate disguise, put on glasses and a false mustache, and flew to a small town in the Urals.

There he met a farmer and said, "Tell me, what do you think of Khrushchev?"

The farmer answered, "Sh-h-h-h ... you crazy or something?"

He looked around furtively and took the Premier inside his farmhouse. He closed all the windows, bolted the doors, pulled down the shades, then whispered, "I like him."

PRAYER

475. *Exceptions*

A Christian farmer was spending a day in a large city. Entering a restaurant for his noon meal, he found a table near a group of young men. When his meal was served. he quietly, with bowed head, gave thanks for the food before him.

The young men, observing this, thought they would

ridicule and embarrass the old gentleman. One called out in a loud voice: "Hey, farmer, does everyone do that where you live?"

The old man looked at the callow youth and calmly said: "No, son, the pigs don't."

PRIDE

476. True *Humility*

A movie idol was a guest at a dinner party, and was surrounded by a company of lovely guests, who drank in every word . . . and his every word was of himself.

For an hour or more he discussed himself, as they sat enraptured. Then in a flash of modesty he said with true humility: "Oh, but we've been talking too much about me. Now, let's talk about you. How did you like my last picture?"

Parade

477. *Eligibility*

The hotel clerk smiled pleasantly at the pompous-looking man who stood at the registration desk and inquired, "What is your name, sir?"

The man, obviously annoyed, gruffly rejoined with, "Don't you see my signature on the register?"

The clerk said, "Yes, sir. That's what aroused my curiosity."

Parade

478. *Cured*

A fellow talking with a friend, both coming out of a psychiatrist's office, said, "I used to be the most conceited, arrogant, egotistical, prideful man you ever saw, until I saw my psychiatrist. Now you just couldn't meet a nicer guy than I am anywhere."

479. *Vanity*

Three women were doing their utmost to impress each other. "My husband bought me a bracelet worth twenty-five thousand dollars," one of them said, "but I had to return it to the jewelers because I am allergic to platinum."

"My husband bought me a mink, costing twenty-five thousand dollars, but I had to return it to the furriers because I am allergic to it," one of the others said.

The third lady fainted. When she regained consciousness the other two asked what caused her to faint. She replied: "It's just that I'm allergic to hot air."

480. *Deflated* Ego

"I've just been made a vice-president of our Company," Jack proudly informed his wife.

"So what!" replied his wife, annoyed with his lack of humility. "Vice-presidents are a dime a dozen. Why, the supermarket where I shop has so many vice-presidents that they have one in charge of prunes."

Troubled by his wife's remark, Jack decided to verify it. He called the supermarket and asked for the vice-president in charge of prunes, and the voice at the other end inquired politely, "Packaged or bulk?"

481. *Ignorance* No Excuse

A big lion was stalking the jungle looking for trouble. He grabbed a tiger and asked, "Who is king of the jungle?"

"You are, O mighty lion," answered the tiger.

The lion then grabbed a bear and asked, "Who is king of the jungle?"

"You are, O mighty lion," answered the bear.

Next the lion met an elephant and asked, "Who is king of the jungle?"

The elephant grabbed him with his trunk and whirled him around and threw him against a tree, leaving him bleeding and broken.

The lion got up feebly and said, "Just because you don't know the answer is no reason for you to get so rough."

Parade

482. *Fast* and Efficient

A village blacksmith, working at his open forge, hammering a whitehot horseshoe, had just finished the shoe and thrown it to the ground to cool.

The local wise guy and busybody walked in at that

moment. He picked up the horseshoe, but dropped it with a howl of pain.

"Pretty hot, eh?" asked the blacksmith.

"Naw," said the wise guy. "It just don't take me long to look over a horseshoe."

483. Out-*boasting* Texas!

A Texan was visiting Niagara Falls.

"I bet you haven't got anything like that in Texas," a local resident said, pointing to the falls.

The Texan, scratching his head said, "No, but we have a plumber in Texas who can stop that leak!"

484. Out-*boasting* Texas

A Kentucky boy was boasting to a visiting Texan about the gold in Fort Knox.

"Here in Kentucky," he said, "we've enough gold to build a solid gold fence, three feet high and two feet wide, all the way around Texas."

"Well, go ahead and build it," said the Texan. "If we like it we'll buy it."

485. *Saving Face*

Squire Perkins bought a calf one day and labored to lead it home with a short rope. For greater safety he tied the rope around his own body. The calf got frightened and obstinate and dragged the worthy squire through a few bramble-bushes, a couple of fences and various other objects of scenery.

Finally, some interested spectators cornered the pair and started to loosen the rope from the squire's waist. He was so nearly out of breath he couldn't say anything for a moment, but he finally gasped out, "Untie the calf; never mind me, I'll stand."

A Bit of Honey

PROFESSIONS

486. Adequate *Rewards*

One chorus girl was talking to another backstage at the end of the performance.

"What's wrong with the leading lady?" asked the first. "She acts mad about something."

"She only got nine bouquets over the footlights," replied the other.

"Nine?" exclaimed the first. "That's pretty good, isn't it?"

"Yeah," drawled her friend, "but she paid for ten."

Parade

487. *Substitution*

The great Maestro, Toscanini, was as well-known for his ferocious temper as for his outstanding musicianship. When members of his orchestra played badly, he would pick up anything in sight and hurl it to the floor.

During one rehearsal a flat note caused the genius to grab his valuable watch and smash it beyond repair.

Shortly afterward, he received from his devoted musicians a luxurious velvet-lined box containing two watches, one a beautiful gold timepiece, the other a cheap one on which was inscribed, "For rehearsals only."

488. Professional *Courtesy*

A lawyer, a doctor and a minister were fishing so intently that they did not notice that their boat had drifted away from the island. Being without oars, they became frantic and drew straws to see who would swim to shore for help.

The lawyer lost and started a straight line for the shore, when he met a line of shark fins cutting off his path. Suddenly, they parted and he swam right through.

The doctor said, "It's a modern miracle."

The minister said, "Miracle nothing, it was a professional courtesy."

489. *Mercy*

A lady took her picture to the photographer, and told him he didn't do her justice.

The photographer replied, "Lady, you don't need justice —you need mercy."

SCHOOL—EDUCATION

490. *Trying*

A schoolmaster had developed a reputation for short reports to parents. On one occasion he wrote on a boy's card: "Trying." The parents were delighted until the next report came. It read, "Very trying!"

491. *Kindness*

The teacher asked the pupils to tell the meaning of loving-kindness. A little boy jumped up and said, "Well, if I was hungry and someone gave me a piece of bread and butter, that would be kindness.

"But if they put a little jam on it, that would be loving-kindness."

492. By *Reputation*

A class of students was watching the professor of chemistry give a demonstration of the properties of various acids. "Now," said the professor, "I am going to drop this half dollar into this glass of acid. Will it dissolve?"

"No sir," replied one of the students.

"No?" said the professor. "Then perhaps you will explain to the class why it won't dissolve."

"Because," came the answer. "If the half dollar would dissolve, you wouldn't drop it in."

F'r Instance

493. Bad *Memory*

"How can you say that I am absent-minded?" the irate professor asked his wife. "My memory is excellent! There are only three things I can't remember. I can't remember names—I can't remember faces—and I can't remember what the third thing is."

494. *Grammatical* Correctness

A young fellow was being raised by very dignified English grandparents in America.

One day a bow-legged cowboy came by, and the boy said, "Hey, look, I ain't never seen nothing like that."

His grandmother said, "Son, I will help you improve

your English," and she bought some Shakespeare books which he began to study.

Later she took the boy to town to see how he had progressed. When he saw a cowboy this time he said, "Hark, what manner of men are these with their legs in parentheses?"

495. In a Big *Rush*

The little boy just couldn't learn. One day his teacher asked him who signed the Declaration of Independence. He didn't know. For almost a week she asked him the same question every day, but still he could not come up with the right answer.

Finally, in desperation, she called the boy's father to her office. "Your boy won't tell me who signed the Declaration of Independence," she complained.

"Come here, son, and sit down," the dad said to the boy. "Now if you signed the crazy thing, admit it and let's get out of here."

496. *Checking* Up

A little boy asked his teacher if a person should be punished for something he hadn't done.

The teacher said, "No, certainly not."

"Good," said the little boy. "I haven't done my arithmetic."

497. In *Agreement*

Little Willie had been in the principal's office so many times that he should have been the assistant principal.

Finally the principal's patience was exhausted. Grabbing the boy by the shoulders and shaking him, he said, "I believe the devil has hold of you, Willie."

"Yes," said Willie, his teeth chattering. "I think so, too, sir."

498. *Justification*

The manager of a theater saw a small boy buying a ticket for the afternoon show. He followed him and said: "Son, why aren't you in school?"

"I don't have to go to school," reported the boy. "I've got the measles."

499. High I. Q.

Little Danny, aged eight, came home with the oft repeated complaint: "Teacher's picking on me again."

"Is that so?" said his mother angrily. "Enough is enough. She's been picking on you all year. Now it's going to stop. Tomorrow, Danny, I'll go to school with you, and we'll have it out with her."

The following morning mother arrived with Danny and demanded an explanation from the teacher.

"That's ridiculous," the teacher replied in answer to the mother's tirade. "Accusing me of picking on your child. I've never picked on any student. Besides," she added, "you might as well know the truth. Your Danny is not very bright, and when I use the word 'bright' I am being excessively kind. Let me show you what I mean."

"Danny" she called. "Tell us how much is five and five?"

"You see, Mom," cried the boy, "she's picking on me again!"

Parade

SPEAKERS—INTRODUCTION

500. *Captive* Audience

"Before I bring my message," a visiting speaker told his somewhat restless audience, "I have one announcement I have been asked to make.

"There is a woman in the hallway who claims that someone in the audience owes her two dollars for laundry. She doesn't wish to embarrass anyone by mentioning their name, but will remain outside for thirty minutes, waiting for her money. If anyone leaves in the next thirty minutes we'll find out who she is waiting for."

501. Speakers *Response*

The meal was over and the Club members were buzzing with conversation and laughter.

The program chairman arose to introduce the guest speaker.

He said, "Let's come to order, members. It's time for the speaker. You can enjoy yourselves some other time."

502. Sudden *Ending*

The speaker for the evening was not only boring, but also long-winded. The fact that the audience kept checking their watches did not seem to phase him in the least. Suddenly the back door flew open and two men entered. One was carrying a rope and the other a shotgun. Startled, the speaker made a hasty conclusion' and sat down.

"Brother, it looks like I just got through in time," he said to the toastmaster, wiping the perspiration from his brow.

The toastmaster replied: "Don't worry, son. They aren't after you. They're after the program chairman."

503. Common *Knowledge*

The speaker made an elegant but rather lengthy speech in the local asylum. When he had finished a man stood up and said, "Mister, your speech was too long."

"Well, I appreciate constructive criticism. Thank you!"

The man didn't sit down, however, but continued by saying, "And you spoke too loud."

The speaker said, "I appreciate that, too. I didn't realize I was speaking that loud."

"Also," replied the man, "you didn't say anything either," and sat down.

The host tried to apologize to the speaker. "That man is a moron, absolutely insane, as a matter of fact, he never says anything that he doesn't hear everyone else around him say."

504. Even *Trade*

The speaker had been addressing his audience for some time, when the microphone went dead.

He raised his voice and asked a man in the back row if he could hear.

"No," was the reply.

Immediately, a man in the front row stood and shouted back, "I can hear and I'll change places with you."

505. *Second* Choice

A women's club had slated a speaker, but at the last

moment she was called away to Atlantic City, leaving them with no other alternative than having one of their own members "pinch hit."

Introducing the speaker and apologizing for the change of program, the chairman said, "Our scheduled speaker was called away to Atlantic City, and I'm sure all of you wish that you were there, too."

506. *Introduction* Response

An after-dinner speaker talked on and on. Finally, one guest whispered to another. "What follows him?"

The other answered: "Thursday."

507. *Ice Breakers* for Speakers

A speaker started his talk by asking all who had heard him at least once, to hold up their hands. Then he said, "All of you hold up your hands that this is the first time you have heard me (as hands go up) and you hope it is the last."

How many Methodists ... Episcopalians ... Christians ... Church of God ... Baptists in this meeting? Well, this place is lousy with Baptists.

A speaker started out by saying to his audience, on a hot evening, "How many had rather be here than in the best air-conditioned jail in the country?"

508. *Speakers*—Sign Posts

The minister prayed, "Lord, fill me with worthwhile stuff, and nudge me when I've said enough."

A sign on the speaker's table read, "Stand up—Speak up —Shut up!"

A sign on a Pulpit read, "What will I preach about?" "About twenty minutes."

A sign on the speaker's table of a Service Club read, "If you don't strike oil in twenty minutes, stop boring."

"They say he is long-winded."
"He may be long—but never winded."

The speaker said, "I was told I can speak as long as I want to . . . but everyone leaves at 9:00 o'clock."

509. Introductions

Before I got married I said I was going to be boss, or know the reason why. I want you to meet the reason why. (Introduce wife).

"I don't know how to introduce our speaker," said the chairman. "He's from Texas, so I suppose he is like one of those Texas cyclones, you don't introduce them, but just get out of their way."

A man was asked who is the boss in your home. "Well, my wife bosses the children, the children boss the dog and cat, and I say anything I like to the geraniums."

510. Flowery Introduction

I feel like a business man who was introduced as a man who had made a hundred thousand dollars in oil in California.

He responded: "There have been several mistakes in this introduction. First, it wasn't in California . . . it was West Virginia. Second, it wasn't oil . . . it was coal. Third, it wasn't me . . . it was my brother, and fourth, it wasn't a hundred thousand he made . . . it was fifty thousand he lost."

511. Introductions-Responses

The toastmaster, after hearing the speaker give a long, lifeless talk, said, "Please keep in mind, ladies and gentlemen, our speaker is speaking free of charge."

I have three women in my family . . . two daughters and one wife. When all of them start working on me, I feel like throwing up my hands and saying, "Lord, give me back my rib."

A Baptist preacher was introduced as a humble Baptist.

The toastmaster said, "Let us see this great thing that has come to pass."

Now I know how buckwheat cakes feel, when the syrup is poured on them.

The introduction had been most flattering. The speaker rose and said: "After an introduction like that, I can hardly wait to hear what I'm going to say."

Your mind begins to work the day you are born and doesn't stop until you get up to make a speech.

STATISTICS

512. *Age*

I'm in the neighborhood of forty, but it's a pretty good-sized neighborhood.

513. *Statistics*

The old gentleman was buying a pair of shoes. He said he didn't think the leather was very good. The salesman said: "The leather in those shoes will last longer than you do."

The elderly gentleman, who was 98, said, "Young man, that's where you're wrong. Statistics show that fewer people die after 98 years of age than at any other age up to that time."

WOMEN

514. **Apparent** *Interest*

The museum guide had patiently shown the visiting Women's Club through the museum.

"Now, ladies, are there any questions you would like to ask?" he said cheerfully.

"Yes," a voice from the group piped up. "Can you tell me the kind of wax you use to keep the floors so shiny?"

515. Simple *Solution*

An old lady took a faded photograph of her late husband to a photographic studio. "Can you make an oil portrait from this snapshot?" she asked.

"Yes, it's possible," said the photographer.

"And could you curl his mustache?" she asked. "And remove the wart from his nose?"

"Yes, it's possible," said the photographer.

"And could you take that hat off his head, so that his lovely black wavy hair shows?" she said.

"Yes, it's possible ma'am, but which side did he part his hair on?" the photographer inquired.

"Oh," said the little old lady, "I can't remember, but you'll find out when you take his hat off!"

516. *Women* Talkers

A scientist rushed into the main control room of the Missile Center at Cape Canaveral and proudly announced a new discovery: "Men" he shouted, "there are women on the moon."

Another scientist asked how he could be sure. Replied the first scientist: "We shot a communications missile up there and got the busy signal."

Parade

517. Point of *View*

A woman was being congratulated by a friend after her son and daughter were married within a month of each other.

"What kind of boy did your daughter marry?" asked the neighbor.

"Oh, he's wonderful," gushed the mother. "He makes her sleep late, wants her to go to the beauty parlor every day, won't let her cook, and insists upon taking her out to dinner every night."

"That's nice," said the neighbor. "And your son? What kind of a girl did he marry?"

The mother sighed, "Oh, I'm not so happy there. She's lazy. Sleeps late every morning, spends all her time at the beauty parlor, won't cook, and makes them take all their meals out."

Parade

518. Modern *Communication*

The leader was pleading with his group to invite people to the special meeting. He said, "Use all means possible—telephone—telegraph—and tell-a-woman. Tell a man something and it goes in one ear and out the other. Tell a woman something and it goes in both ears and out her mouth."

519. *Value* Received

A vagrant approached a lady on the street and asked, "Ma'am, would you please give me fifteen cents for a sandwich?"

To which the lady replied, "Let me see the sandwich."

520. *Peace* At Any Cost

Two old women, for an hour or more, battled over whether or not the train window at their seat should be open.

"I'll die of pneumonia if it is," one said.

"I'll die of suffocation, if it's not," the other said.

At last, a very much bored man in the seat across the aisle, suggested to the conductor: "Why don't you open it till one gets pneumonia, and then close it till the other suffocates. Then we'll have peace."

521. Never *Satisfied*

It has been estimated that women have 90 per cent of the world's wealth; still they go through their husband's pockets to get the other 10 per cent.

INDEX

(Numbers after titles refer to number of story)

FOR YOUR READING PLEASURE

EXTRAORDINARY LIVING FOR ORDINARY MEN by Sam Shoemaker
One of America's outstanding churchmen shows how you can lead an extraordinary life—with the faith that turns the commonplace into an exalted reflection of God.
No. 10778p

HOW TO WIN OVER WORRY by John Edmund Haggai
A practical formula for successful living. Shows how to increase your income, handle criticism, improve your health, deal effectively with people, have peace in the midst of trouble.
No. 9740p

THE ART OF UNDERSTANDING YOURSELF by Cecil Osborne
A powerfully written self-help book that combines psychology and religion as an aid for richer and happier living.
No. 10472p

MANAGING YOUR TIME by Ted W. Engstrom and Alex Mackenzie
Practical suggestions to make the most of yourself . . . and your day. As valuable as an extra hour in the day for the housewife, businessman, student.
No. 9572p

DOES ANYONE HERE KNOW GOD? by Gladys Hunt
Dynamic true stories of 17 women whose lives changed after encountering God and His love, among them: Eleanor Searle Whitney, Jane Stuart Smith, Yoshiko Taguchi, Betty Carlson.
No. 9880p

A TREASURY OF HUMOR by Clyde Murdock
An uproarious collection of more than 500 jokes, puns, anecdotes and humorous stories . . . for all occasions. Conveniently categorized, the subjects are arranged alphabetically for ease of use.
No. 10368p

ENCYCLOPEDIA OF GAMES by Doris Anderson
Choice collection of 686 games in wholesome fun . . . for all occasions and every season . . . many never in print before . . . a boon for youth group leaders and every parent.
No. 9076p

HOW TO MAKE A HABIT OF SUCCEEDING by Mack R. Douglas
Practical guide to harnessing the power of purpose and the might of motivation to produce dynamic action . . . by a man who has applied and improved upon Dale Carnegie's methods.
No. 9536p

THE GOSPEL BLIMP by Joseph Bayly
Reach and inspire with faith one billion people?—with a blimp??? They tried . . . the result: a searching, moving hilarious parable of Christian purpose gone astray . . . a modern masterpiece now in its 5th big printing.
No. 12288p

PRAYER: CONVERSING WITH GOD by Rosalind Rinker
A dynamic explanation of conversational prayer, the spiritual strength it brings and the inner rewards of awaiting His reply . . . 17 printings to date in hardcover . . . "the best, direct, understandable book on prayer"—Baptist Sunday School Board.
No. 10716p

DARE TO LIVE NOW! by Bruce Larson
Shows how life can be changed now for anyone who knows how to appropriate the power and love of God through Christ and presents concretely the how of faith—how to lay hold of God's willingness to help, to heal and to guide in everyday life situations.
No. 10001p